TOTAL QUALITY ASSESSMENT IN INSURANCE

DR. STEWARD DOSS
&
DR. V.S. KAVERI

2000
AKANSHA PUBLISHING HOUSE
NEW DELHI

Published by
Akansha Publishing House
R 37-B, Vani Vihar, Uttam Nagar
New Delhi-110059

Total Quality Assessment in Insurance

First Edition 2000

ISBN 81-87606-03-7

Printed in India

Published by M.P.Misra for Akansha Publishing House, New Delhi, Laser Typesetting by Vinayak Computers, Shahdara, Delhi and Printed at Tarun Offset Press, Delhi.

ACKNOWLEDGMENTS

We remain indebted to all those who helped us in bringing out this book. In particular, we are deeply thankful to Sri M.P. Misra, M/s Akansha Publishing house, New Delhi in brining out the book timely and elegantly, Lastly, we wish to express our sincere appreciation of our family members for their support, encouragement and sacrifice while writing the book.

Dr. Steward Doss
Dr. V.S. Kaveri

ACKNOWLEDGMENTS

PREFACE

In the context of liberalization of insurance business in India, Service Quality as a criterion of success is gaining more importance. The exiting as well as potential players in insurance market are expected to meet the global Service-Quality standards. In this regard, the first task is to assess the present level of service-quality. But the required tool for measurement of service quality is not available. Hence, any attempt made to develop the service quality is always appreciated. Keeping this felt need in mind, we have attempted to develop the Service Quality Index for Life Insurance business on the basis of the study of customer's behavioral responses. The present book discusses the concept and process of the Service Quality Index besides offering suggestions for improving the overall quality of life insurance business. Hence, this may be considered as a useful document providing guidelines to officials concerning the insurance business, both life and general, in explaining importance of Service-Quality, knowing the methodology to develop Service Quality Index and understanding suggestions for improving the customer service. Further, this may prove to be a good reference book to the students of M.Com, M.B.A etc. on Service Quality in insurance business. The researchers working on a topic relating to Insurance Business may find this as a source of guidance. Finally, this would be a good library reference book.

PREFACE

CONTENTS

CONTENTS

Chapter 1

IMPACT OF LIBERALIZATION OF THE INSURANCE SECTOR ON CUSTOMER SERVICE

The origin of the Insurance Regulatory and Development Bill, 1999

When the decision was taken almost eight years ago to liberalize the Indian economy, the expert committees recommended to overhaul the entire financial structure- direct taxes, indirect taxes, banking, capital markets and insurance. All recommendations of these committees except insurance have been given effect to, with modifications as suggested by the standing Parliamentary Committees. Subsequently, the Malhotra Committee report of the insurance sector reform was submitted in 1994 but successive Governments did not show much interest in implementing it. It was only in 1997 that the United Front Government introduced the Insurance Regulatory and Development Bill which was opposed by the employees of the Life Insurance Corporation (LIC) and General Insurance Corporation (GIC), and opposition parties namely, the two communist parties, Samajwadi party and Bharthiya Janata Party

(BJP). The Bill was opposed on the ground that, on liberalization foreign insurance companies would enter into the field, strangle the public sector giant corporations and throw out the present employees. The opposition parties were so vehement in their arguments that the consideration of the Bill that the Parliament preferred to refer it to the Parliamentary Committee. Ironically, the BJP led government was the first one to introduce in early 1998 a revised Bill, which had emanated from the Parliamentary Committee. As the twelfth Lok Sabha was dissolved, the consideration of the Bill was lapsed. But recently, the same lapsed Bill was reintroduced and is now approved by the Parliament.

Features of the Bill The Insurance Regulatory and Development Bill, 1999 seeks to open up the insurance sector to private and foreign investors. As per the Bill, new entrants, who must be Indian, will be granted license to transact insurance business only if they introduce a minimum capital of Rs. 100 crores for life and general insurance business and Rs. 200 crores for reinsurance business. Foreign collaboration will be allowed but foreign investment is capped at 26 percent of the total capital. The Insurance Regulatory Authority and Development (IRDA) is vested with powers to disallow entry of foreign investors through subterfuges such as the NBFC collaboration route. Though solvency margins of Rs. 50 crore for life, Rs. 50 crore or a sum equivalent to 20 percent of net premium collection for general insurance and Rs. 100 crore for reinsurance are prescribed. The Bill requiring separate accounts to be maintained for funds of shareholders and policy holders, directs that the policy holders' funds should be retained within the country.

Challenges of the Liberlized Market

The liberalised market environment envisages numerous challenges for the existing as well as new players in the market. Some of them are given below:

Market convergence: The financial reform in India has already triggered integration of Financial Institutions, Banks, and Asset Management Companies. Now, the entire financial market is converging as a result of insurance liberalization. Banking and Financial Institutions have indicated their interest in entering into insurance. Similarly, the insurance companies have also revealed their desire for banking business. In the developed markets, the convergence has already taken place, as a result of which an integrated financial regulatory body known as 'the International Association of Insurance Supervisors' has been established by combining together the regulations of Securities, Banking and Insurance. India also would be witnessing the same very soon. In the coming years, the market boundary would be lifted off and with the booming off e-commerce and technology convergence, there will be a single market the world over.

Treatment of Business: The Regulatory Authority has made it clear that the business of life, non-life and reinsurance would be treated as separate business. The companies have to maintain separate books of accounts for life, non-life, and reinsurance respectively. Companies would be allowed to enter into other fields, but they have to get a separate license for each business.

Widening of product line: The opening up of the market would bring more and more new products in insurance. There will be an increasing demand for variable and unit-linked insurance products. These products would have a high liquidity and offer a better return. More innovative and hi-tech products will also be available. Thus, the insurance product-lines would get widened. A single company would be offering insurance, pension, health, banking, and securities/bonds to a customer. The product competition will demand the companies to match global standards in product quality.

Service Quality: In such an environment, the service quality will become the global mantra for survival and to be a market leader. The world over, it has enabled the companies to attain operational efficiency, greater financial performance, product/service differentiation, and competitive edge. When quality has already become a primary corporate objective in manufacturing and service sectors, particularly among the private companies in India, insurance companies still have long way to go in this process. But, the new market would demand for matching global quality standards in the key process areas, such as underwriting, systems, employee's performance, services of operating office, agent's services, business performance, etc.

Technological impact: The companies would become technology driven as it is proved to be a key to provide competitive edge. Knowledge management system, total computerisation, Intranet, Internet, and e-commerce applications will gain a significant importance. In this regard, the following are some of the issues concerning the Insurance Regulator:

(i) Legality of digital and electronic signature, electronic fund transfer, electronic application, premium collection by credit card, privacy and confidentiality issues.

(ii) Approval of the System for Electronic Rates and Forms Filing (SERFF) to create the electronic filing environment for the filing of rates and forms.

(iii) Regulation for doing insurance business through e-commerce, selling insurance products on the Internet, guidelines for advertisement.

(iv) Guidelines regarding geographical boundary, ensuring the insurer or producer has appropriate license to transact business in the place where the consumer is located.

(v) Legal issues concerning the electronically transmitted insurance applications, policies, and related forms - whether they have the same legal equivalent of the paper-based forms.

Re-structuring: The liberalized market might witness many companies going in for restructuring which may take place through joint ventures, mergers, internal restructuring of product lines, systems, distribution channel, investment portfolios, etc. Companies may prefer to follow the best practices in every key processes, which may see out-sourcing of certain processes (the insurance companies may out-source the distribution of simple products to banks which, in-turn, out-source underwriting to insurance companies), franchising for selling certain products, Internet selling, and e-commerce. LIC has indicated its desire to have joint ventures to sell pension products, to enter into Banking and Health insurance, while the other financial institutions such as State Bank of India, ICICI, HDFC, etc., have already shown their willingness to enter into insurance with the help of foreign partners. High order of structural conglomeration may become necessity. Entry of multi-nationals in the insurance sector may cause the Indian companies to go into mergers and joint ventures to compete against the giant multinationals.

Multi-channel Distribution: Under this liberalized market, many companies might go in for multiple channels of distribution. E-Commerce is another area for insurance business. Corporate bodies, institutions, and co-operative societies may be allowed to sell the insurance policies. The technological developments, which have already affected banks and other financial institutions, may soon create a direct impact on insurance sector also. At the initial stage, there will be greater competition among the companies in tapping the cream of the market (rich and high middle segment) might possibly be approached regularly by direct marketing through mail, telephone, and Internet. The direct selling may grow at slightly faster rate, as many of the Indian co-porates such as ICICI, IDBI, HDFC, etc., which are having a strong base in this segment and with their foreign partners who already have a regular enough experience and expertise in this direct marketing, may prefer this channel, apart from agents, brokers, and consultants, to have regular contact with their clients. The main advantage of this direct channel, besides being low cost, would be its suitability to strengthen their customer relationship. This also could be a very good tool for Relationship Marketing.

Maintaining Profit Margin: The companies would be under pressure to maintain the targeted profit margin. This may involve the following:

Maximizing the mobilization of savings from the targeted segments,

Greater care in the shuffling of portfolios for the approved investments,

Developing a cost control mechanism,

Control over the price-cutting, incentives, and premium discounts to increase the market share.

Periodical review of asset-liability to ensure appropriate asset allocation, holding of good quality of assets, and liquid and remunerative loan portfolio

Cost-benefit control for each product periodically to ensure a profitable product mix.

Consumer Protection: Under the liberalized market, the regulatory authority has more responsibility to protect the customer's interest, particularly from the possibility of insolvency of the companies. In other Asian markets where the liberalization has already been made, many companies have become insolvent mainly due to more liberal regulation and stricter supervision and economic slow-down, which caused fears among the policyholders. Though the insurance reform in India is expected to be more comprehensive and transparent than the other Asian countries, the stricter regulatory norms to protect the interest of policyholders are called for. The same is needed in the following areas;

(i) claim settlement,

(ii) repudiation of claims,

(iii) nature of businesses of both private and public sector,

(iv) payment of bonus,

(v) regulating the intermediaries from unfair trade practices, wrong selection of policies, sufficient disclosure of product information inadequate product knowledge, providing regular satisfactory services, etc.

(vi) promoting the insurers to do adequate customer-education,

(vii) inspection of insurers to ensure operational efficiency and cost control.

(viii) minimizing the possibility of insolvency of the companies,

(ix) continuous monitoring and periodical checking of the capital adequacy and solvency margins of the insurers,

(x) establishing a rating agency similar to 'CAMELS' rating (An integrated rating of Capital, Assets, Management, Earnings, Liquidity, and System).

(xi) ensuring the policyholders that the insurance companies are earning a good return and providing a competitive return.

Price War: Intensive market competition would result in a price war, which might possibly lower the premium rates either by way of price cutting or offering more benefits such as of better return, high liquidity, additional bonus, etc. In the Asian Pacific and European markets, the premium rates went down substantially because, the companies mainly concentrated on increasing their market share. Since the insurance premium may be determined by market players including insured, insurance companies and reinsures, there is a need for strict regulation on the part of IRDA to ensure that the price cutting does not affect the company's net worth, competition, quality of products \ services, etc.

Greater Market Growth: As an outcome of liberlization, insurance business is expected to witness an impressive growth. As per the estimates of market survey, the insurance coverage would increase to 30% by 2003 from the present level of 15%. This would translate into business worth of $10.5 billion. According to a study, about 80% of India's insurable population is as yet untapped which represents a tremendous business opportunity in the coming times. Thus, the opening-up of the insurance sector will expand the size of the market significantly. At least 20 - 25 companies in the private sector have already expressed their willingness to enter into the market.

Growth of Rural Business: The IRDA Act, 1999 stipulates 'Every insurer shall, after the commencement of the Insurance Regulatory and Development Authority Act, 1999, undertake such percentage of life insurance business and general insurance business in the rural or social sector as may be specified, in the official gazette by the Authority, in this behalf". This would certainly improve the rural business. The Government owned insurance companies (LIC & GIC) have a strong presence in the rural sector, and have a sizable reputation also; Hence for the new players, it will be difficult to penetrate into rural areas. Thus, they may prefer to do selective and lucrative business in urban areas. This may give a strong hand for LIC and GIC in improving their market share in the rural areas. Similarly, State Bank of India and Nationalised Banks which are having substantial capital strength, extensive network, and significant financial trust among the people, have also shown their desire to enter into rural sector, ensures a greater rural growth.

Capital Adequacy and Solvency Margin: The market would demand for the companies to have a strong capital-base, which can provide a protection against adverse performance and flexibility to respond to market changes. Every insurer shall maintain excess assets over liabilities. In this regard, certain points shall be kept in mind. For instance, in the case of an insurer carrying on life insurance business, the required solvency margin shall be higher than of the following;

(a) Fifty crores of rupees (Rs.100 crores in case of re-insurers); or

(b) The aggregate sum of the results shall be arrived at in items (i) & (ii) stated below:-

(i) the aggregate of the results arrived at by applying the calculation described under item (A) below(step I) and the calculation described under item (B) below(step II):

(A) Step I

(A.1) there shall be taken, a sum equal to a percentage determined by regulations not exceeding 5% of the mathematical reserves for direct business and re-insurance acceptances without any deduction for re-insurance cessions;

(A. 2) the amount of mathematical reserves at the end of the preceding financial year after the deduction of re-insurance cessions shall be expressed as a percentage of the amount of those mathematical reserves before any such deduction; and

(A. 3) the sum mentioned under item (A. I) shall be multiplied-

(A.3.1) where the percentage arrived at under item (A. 2) above is greater than eighty-five percent. (or in the case of a re-insurer carrying on exclusive re-insurance business, fifty percent.), by that greater percentage; and

(A.3.2) in any other case, by eighty-five percent. (or in the case of a re-insurer carrying on exclusive re-insurance business, fifty percent);

(B) Step II

(B. 1) there shall be taken, a sum equal to a percentage determined by the regulations made by the Authority not exceeding one percent of the sum at risk for the policies on which the sum at risk is not a negative figure, and

(B.2) the amount of sum at risk at the end of the preceding financial year for policies on which the sum at risk is not a negative figure after the deduction of re-insurance cession shall be expressed as a percentage of the amount of that sum at risk before any such deduction, and

(B. 3) the sum arrived at under item(B 3.1) above shall be multiplied

(B. 3.1) where the percentage arrived at under item (B. 2) above is greater than fifty percent, by that greater percentage; and

(B. 3.2) in any other case, by fifty percent.

(ii) the percentage determined by the regulations made by the Authority of the value of assets determined in accordance with the provisions of section 64V;

The above solvency norms provide the insurers a stiff norms to be maintained under the competitive market. Further, there is a provision that the regulatory authority has full powers to increase the margin requirements if it is not satisfied with the quality of an insurer's assets. In case of each insurer, the IRDA has the powers to examine the claims to premium ratio. If the IRDA is convinced that the premium corpus is insufficient to meet the expected claims, it will be able to revise the solvency margin upwards. It is expected that the solvency margin likely to be pegged at five times the net owned funds of an insurance company.

Prudent Investment: Under high volatility of primary market, continuous improvements in the investment strategy through appropriate shuffling of asset-mix, asset-liability management and mark to market asset valuation are indispensable.

Impact of the Liberalization of the Insurance Sector

The Bill does not envisage the privatization of the LIC and GIC. This does not limit anywhere that these corporations will be dismantled. Though it will be as usual business for them, there will be competition from private insurance companies that are going to be set up soon. In this regard, banks, financial institutions, business houses and foreign investors have already expressed their readiness to enter into the insurance sector. Though there is no threat of loss of employment in LIC and GIC, employee of these corporations have to change themselves in view of the fierce competition emerging from the private insurance companies.

It is felt that the LIC and GIC will lose the business on opening up of the insurance sector. But this is not so provided the quality of the service is exceedingly good. Similarly, the range of products should be sufficiently large and customer friendly. In any case, both corporations have to struggle to retain and expand the present business.

There are a few more apprehensions of the two corporations. For instance, it is felt that the private operations have certain facilities that are not available with them. To elaborate, in spite of the provisions to transact a certain percentage of business in the rural and social sectors, the private operators may not only capture the cream of the business in urban centers but also make an impressive entry in the rural areas. Secondly, the private insurance companies may offer several incentives and quote low rates. Further, the private entrants may attract the talented professional managers from these two corporations by offering an attractive pay-package. It is also felt that, though both the corporations have a wide network of branches and are adequately equipped in terms of infrastructure, they are lacking in autonomy to run business on commercial basis.

Insurance business potential in India is unlimited. To elaborate, insurance coverage in India is 12.4 per 1000 people as compared to 35 in Malayasia and 198 in Japan. In the Life Insurance business, there are only 45 million insured persons out of nearly a billion eligible population in India and there is scope for increasing this to 250 million in another five years. It is estimated that insurance business in India for 2001-2002 would be the 80000 crores. If so much is business potential, what is required is to attract customers by understanding their expectations and making arrangements to meet the same.

Customers' Expectations: To tap this increasing business potential, it is important to introduce customer friendly services. To elaborate, a spate of deaths arising from violence, accidents and havoc caused by nature have created a greater awareness of life insurance among the people. The same applies to the general insurance sector also where fire, accident and motor vehicle insurance's have compensated for damaged or wrecked property. Today, customers i.e. policyholders expect only one comprehensive policy to cover life insurance, accident insurance and health care. They also expect that insurance companies should introduce a 'cradle to the grave' insurance policy. They certainly welcome the services at the doorstep and at affordable costs. The more important for them is to receive the services promptly and under the computerized environment. Since India is a vast country, there should be flexibility in operations so that insurance companies can accommodate the local requirements. Above all, there should be a professional approach in satisfying their needs. So, companies, which will enjoy a competitive edge in meeting customers' needs, will certainly prosper.

Need for Total Quality Assessment Model

In the above bank-drop, it is essential for every insurance company to assess the quality of its services from time to time. For assessment of the service quality, suitable tools in the form of Total Quality Assessment Models have to be developed. Since such models are not readily available, any attempt made in developing the same is appreciated. In this book, a modest attempt is made to explain the concept and process of the Total Quality Assessment Models with special reference to Life Insurance in India.

Chapter 2

AN OUTLINE OF THE STUDY

Importance of Quality

The world-over, 'Quality' has enabled industries to make turn-around by setting new benchmarks. It is considered as a tool to achieve total customer satisfaction. Its importance is realized in most of the developed countries such as USA, Germany, Sweden, NewZealand, etc., where a national quality or customer satisfaction index is developed for the evaluation of national economy. The European Union also has recommended it for its member countries[1]. Such index evaluates and enhances the performance of firms, industries, economic sectors, and national economies. In India too, many companies have now shifted their focus from 'Productivity to Quality' which can be evidenced from their use Total Quality Management (TQM), Business Process Re-engineering (BPR), ISO 9000 Certification, etc., as a method to improve the quality.

The 'Quality Revolution' has spread through manufacturing industries to service industries as customers have begun to demand for better level of performance. Consequently, many companies in India are using new marketing techniques such as DataBase Marketing, Relationship Marketing, and Techno-Marketing, to give a customized service for their customers. For instance, Air-India, Indian Airlines, Indian Tobacco Company, Nestle, Lotus, Lever India, Philips etc., are using 'Data Base Marketing' to understand the individual customer's preferences to offer a need based service. Similarly, Modi Xerox, HCL-HP, DHL, Grindlays, Bank of America, City Bank, etc., are using 'Relationship Marketing' to offer personalized services. And, Indian Rayon, Laxmi India, Reebok, Mafatlal, Ceat Tyres, Birla Cements, etc., are trying to sell their products by offering technical consultancy services through their own retail outlets at free of cost for their customers, explaining them about the technical aspects of their products, how to use their products in a better way, and providing the customized service to each customer under 'Techno-Marketing'[2].

Thus, the Customer Satisfaction has become a key differentiator wherever the market is highly competitive. Major companies including multi-national companies such as Levers India, Cadburys India, Videocon, Modi Xerox, Wipro Infotech, Mafatlal Industries, Britannia, City Bank, Tafe, HCL-HP India, American Express, Mahindra and Mahindra, have focused their attention on customer satisfaction and orientation of their employees towards customer service.

But, this scenario makes it interesting to know why suddenly the service quality or customer satisfaction has become so important for all sectors; does the cost of quality improvement fetch any return? In this context, Forenell (1992)[3] enumerates several benefits of high customer satisfaction to a firm. In general, high customer satisfaction should indicate the increased loyalty for current customers, reduced price elasticity, insulation of current customers from competitive efforts, lower cost of future transactions, reduced failure costs, lower cost of attracting new customers and enhanced reputation for the firm. These significant features profound quality approach (TQM, BPR, ISO 9000, etc.) in almost all the industries.

Need for defining Service Quality

The term 'Service Quality' has been considered as an abstract concept, and is more difficult to measure. It is often related with good's quality, goodness, excellence, greater value, aesthetics, etc. Quality and its requirements are not easily articulated by customers (Takeuchi and Quelch 1980)[4]. The inherent distinctive features of the service viz., intangibility, variability and inseparability also make it distinctive from good's quality, and even fair knowledge of manufacturing product's quality, however, is insufficient to understand the service quality. Since services are the performances rather than objects, precise manufacturing specifications concerning uniform quality can rarely be set, and most services can not be counted, measured, inventoried, tested and verified in advance of sale to ensure quality (Bateson 1977, Shostak 1977, Berry 1980, and Lovelock 1981)[5]. Secondly, because of the variability nature, consistency of behavior from service personnel (i.e. uniform quality) is difficult to ensure; what the firm intents to deliver may be entirely different from what the customers receive (Booms and Bitner 1981)[6]. Thirdly, the inseparability of production and consumption of many services makes it unable to be engineered at the manufacturing plant, and then delivered intact to the customers (Carmen and Langeard 1980, Gronroos 1978, Rogan 1963, Upah 1980)[7]. Moreover, the quality occurs during the service delivery, usually in an interaction between the client and the contact person from the service firm which makes the service firms to have less managerial control over quality (Lehtinen and Lehtinen 1982).[8] These problems make the service companies find it difficult to understand how customers perceive their services and evaluate service quality(Zeithaml 1981)[9].

Therefore, in this study, an attempt has been made to define the term service quality in a more simplistic and understandable way and to assess its applicability in life insurance business.

Challenges for Life Insurance Companies

The life insurance market in India is in transition towards a competitive free market, as the result of new IRDA Act, 1999, which allows the private and foreign players to enter into insurance. Further, the Government's introduction of two other important Bills viz. Information Technology Bill, 1999, and Telecommunication Bill, 1999, assures a much more economy liberalization. This really makes the customer's expectations further heightening. This scenario presents numerous challenges for the insurance companies. These include:

- Customers, today, are income-rich but time-poor, so they expect that, after sales services should be discharged quickly as a matter of their right.
- Many customers perceive the life insurance policies more as a financial product rather than risk cover. So, they would expect the insurance companies to assure competitive returns and more liquidity. Besides, the companies will have to provide more value-added services. Their expectations would pressure them to continue to excel in their services; otherwise there is a

possibility of policyholders switching over to the other organizations if services are poor.

- New competitive environment will force quality competition among the companies, which would force them in setting new bench markets. This requires continuous measurement of their key service areas.

- Now, the customers will have many companies selling life insurance policies, the companies have to provide service differentiation to get competitive advantage.

- A proposal to buy an insurance policy covers occupies a low priority in customers' financial-planning, as the benefits are contingent on certain events occurring. A Life policy might have been bought due to agent's compulsion. So, any poor quality of service may result in lapsation of policy.

- The market boundary is getting lifted off as the result of convergence of market as well as technology. The companies would try to attract the customers with sophisticated technological know-how and expertise. These developments would compel the companies to match Global Quality Standards.

- There will be an intensive competition among the intermediaries i.e. Agents, Brokers, Consultants, etc., in attracting the rich and high middle class customer segments. This will demand for real professionalism among the agents, which the companies might have to ensure.

- Under this competitive market, the customer's loyalty will be short-lived, and attracting the new customers would be costly. So, the companies need to design effective loyalty programs to retain their existing customers and also to attract the new customers.

These challenges will demand the companies to go for Total Quality Assessment to ensure continuous improvement in their key business areas. The total quality assessment requires a customer-based measurement system, because, service quality at the operating offices may be good and delivered within the service specifications. Yet, some customers may perceive it as unsatisfactory, because the same level of quality may be perceived differently by each customer. Therefore, in this study, the total quality in life insurance has been assessed through customers' perceptions.

Life insurance requires a triangle management of Product, Agent, and Office to deliver satisfactory services to the customers, and more importantly, the parameters of service quality: product satisfaction, agent's service, and office service are inter-related. Therefore, to understand the relationship of these variables and service quality, *a service quality model incorporating the linear relationships among these variables of service quality* has been felt necessary to be developed. This would help the companies to understand, monitor and improve their total service quality.

Assessing the total quality in life insurance would be a very complex and difficult task, if the key factors determining the satisfaction of the products and services were not known. So, this study measures *customer satisfaction of the key parameters of service quality (Product, Agent's service and Office service), and identifies the factors determining the satisfaction of these parameters.* This would help understand how customers evaluate the total service quality, and what factors are significant to determine their satisfaction.

In this study, the total service quality has been defined as *'totality of all features and characteristics of products, services, systems and people that gives complete satisfaction'*. This demand for measuring the service quality in totality through customers' perceptions using multiple measures: Product, Agent's service, Office service, and over-all service. For this purpose, a linearly weighted composite index has been created for measuring the 'total service quality' in life insurance.

The available literature on this subject indicates that the relationships of service quality and customer's behavioural responses are very complex and difficult to understand as equal numbers of studies have found this relationship as either linear or non-linear (Customers' behavioural response refers to 'the intended responses of customers to the perceived service quality of a firm i.e. word-of-mouth communications, repurchase, preference, company image, and retention). In India, particularly in life insurance, no such study has been done. The relationship also appears to be depending upon the nature of market i.e. monopolistic or competitive. Under the monopolistic market conditions, the loyalty is expected to be false loyalty because there is no alternatives available. But, in a competitive market the customer loyalty will be short-lived, while under the semi-competive conditions - it will be relatively longer. Now, when the life insurance market is shifting towards semi-competitive environment, it will be worthwhile to study whether the relationship between service quality and customer loyalty is linear or not? Further, there are two different perceptions about the impact of service quality on Life Insurance business: one view is (a) LIC would continue to be monopolistic in nature at least for some time, because it will take quite some time for the new companies to attack LIC, so, service quality may not have greater impact on life insurance business; and the alternative perception is (b) the market is competitive even now, so the service quality would certainly have greater impact on life insurance business. This makes it interesting and essential *to study whether service quality has any measurable impact on life insurance business.* In this study, the impact of service quality has been measured through customers' behavioral responses for the following reasons: I) Customer's behavioral response is a good indicator of future business, so, measuring the impact of service quality on this count, is as good as measuring its effect on the business performances, ii) it is not possible to measure the impact of service quality directly on life insurance business at one time, as it requires to be studied over a period of time.

Earlier Studies

The review of the studies* already done in this area reveals that quality is a holistic concept, all characteristics of products and services together determine quality. Quality does not result from the output only as services evolve in interaction with the customers; all factors become important determinants. They also suggest that quality lies in customer's perception and it should be measured using all the important factors as perceived by them. Further, these studies have stressed a need for measuring the effect of service quality on customers' behavioral responses.

However, the studies already conducted on service quality may be found inadequate in insurance industry. To elaborate, studies conducted, thus far, have mainly focused on measuring the service quality through some selected parameters only. In particular, in Life Insurance, no study has been done for measuring service quality in totality, and it's impact on Life Insurance business. In India also, no such studies have been done so far. Finally, there is an absence of well-established index available to measure the perceived service quality in totality, and the existing studies are also silent in this regard. Therefore, the present study is undertaken to fill up the gap in the literature regarding the vital aspects of the service quality in insurance industry.

About the present study

This study covers:

- *Development of a service quality model explaining the linear relationships among the parameters of service quality;*
- *Measurement of customer satisfaction of the key parameters of service quality and identification of factors determining the satisfaction of these parameters;*
- *Development of a linearly weighted composite index incorporating the linear relationship of service quality to measure service quality at the operating offices of LIC. This index would also capture the relationship of service quality and loyalty; and*
- *Measuring the impact of service quality on customers' behavioral responses.*

Objectives of the study

- To develop a service quality model to study the linear relationships of service quality parameters in life insurance,

- To measure customer satisfactions of the key service quality parameters, and identify the factors determining the satisfaction of these parameters,
- To create an index for measuring the service quality in totality at the operating offices of LIC,
- To assess the impact of service quality on the customers' behavioral responses, and
- To offer suggestions for improvement of service quality in life insurance business.

Methodology

Data Collection

The data were collected on the followings;

- Agent's pre-sales service measures,
- Product satisfaction measures and the factors influencing the same,
- Agent's after-sales service measures,
- Office service measures,
- Over-all service quality measures,
- Measures of customers' behavioral responses: word of mouth, repurchase, preference, company image and retention.
- Personal details of the policyholders: sex, age, occupation, income and insurance experience.
- Policy details: type of policy, term, mode, amount of sum assured, and premium.
- Particulars of the branches selected.
- Views of executives, servicing staff, and agents of LIC on Life Insurance policy servicing.

Sources of Data

(a) Primary Data

- The primary data were collected from the policyholders, agents, servicing staff, and executives of LIC.
- For the selection of various aspects of insurance services both Agent's service as well as Office service, discussions were held with the agents and the servicing staff of the selected branches. Then, the discussions were also held with the executives of various cadres in LIC: Assistant Administrative Officers, Administrative Offices, Branch Managers, Divisional Managers, and Zonal Managers in LIC. These discussions, and also the survey of literature on this subject, helped to identify the necessary data for the study.
- Observations on various aspects of the functioning of LIC, were gained through personal visits to the branch offices, attending the training programs on life insurance, and interactions with the trainees attending the training program's conducted at the National Insurance Academy, Pune. These observations were documented which helped in developing a fair understanding of service quality in LIC.

(b) Secondary Data

- The secondary data were collected from the following sources:
- Selected books, articles, and research papers on service quality, life insurance, and statistics, available in India as well as obtained from other countries.

- Reports of the various study groups appointed by the government to study the working of LIC, and internal reports i.e. annual reports, inspection reports, business performance reports, etc.
- Office servicing procedures and manuals available in the operating offices of LIC, and Agent's manuals.

(c) Collection of Data

(a) ***Data Collection Tool:*** For collecting the data, a structured questionnaire was developed. The questionnaire mainly covers the following:

- Reasons for the purchase of life insurance policies, customers' satisfactions of the policies in meeting their macro insurance needs, cost of the policy, return, safety, and liquidity aspects of the policy; Pre-sales services of agents such as selection of policy, explaining the policy benefits, financial counseling, friendliness, etc.; After-sales services of agents i.e. review of insurance needs, issue of policy documents and premium notices, remittance of premiums, etc. It also covers the various dimensions of office services such as tangibles, accessibility, competence, communication, assurance, responsiveness, reliability, empathy, etc., besides the behavioral responses of the customers i.e. word-of-mouth recommendations, repurchase, preference, company image, and retention. Further, it also includes personal details of the policyholders i.e. sex, age, occupation, income, insurance experience, etc.; and policy details such as type of the policy, term, and mode of payment.

The questionnaire was finalized after conducting a pilot study of a sample consisting of 35 policyholders in one of the branches of Pune Division. After the pilot study, few questions were found to be difficult to understand and therefore, they were restated (A copy of the questionnaire is given in Appendix II).

(b) Selection of Branches

In LIC, the branch offices are the service centers for policyholders. So, these branches become the sampling units for the study. For the purpose of data collection of the study, three Urban Branches in Pune Division in Maharashtra, and one Rural Branch from Madurai Division in Tamil Nadu, were selected, keeping in view of the following criteria:

The urban areas account for nearly 60% of LIC's business, and the rest 40% is from rural areas. Hence, the selection of branches was in accordance with the business quota, and secondly it also covers the regional differences (urban and rural),

The urban branches were selected from Pune city mainly because it is considered as the one of the main centres of trade and commerce, having a large number of educational institutions and with greater rate of literacy (81% in urban).

The Paramakudi Branch (rural branch) in Madurai District was selected for the following reasons: i) It was easy to conduct the interviews with the respondents in the local language; ii) This area is mainly agriculture oriented and has very low industrial and educational development; iii) This branch represents typical rural culture covering large areas and has successful business records over long years. Thus, the four branches selected for the study are of different types:

(i) Conventional Branch,

(ii) Career Agents Branch (Professional Agency Force),

(iii) SSS Branch (Servicing maximum numbers .of Salary Savings Scheme),

(iv) Rural Branch.

The profile of these branches is given below in brief :

(i) *Conventional Branch:* This branch holds a steady and successful record of business performance over a long period, and it is one of the oldest branches in the Division. Most of its functions are computerised.

(ii) *Career Agents Branch:* This branch has exclusively career agents who are professional and well trained. Its functions are not computerised, but it has a computer support from the nearest branches.

(iii) *SSS Branch:* This branch has a large number of policyholders under the salary savings scheme (SSS) which account for more than 70% of its business. This is also one of the oldest branches and is fully computerised.

(Iv) *Rural Branch:* It is one of the high performance branches in terms of business, and having a large area of operations in the Division. But, it is not a fully computerised branch.

(C) Data collection

For collection of data from each of the above selected branches, it was attempted to pick-up a sample size of 100 - 150 policy holders who had received after-sales services during the year 1996-97, by using random sampling method, with an assumption that those who had experienced the service recently (max. one year duration) could only share their recent experiences (perception of a service which had been received two or more years earlier may not be a reliable indicator of current service quality). In the urban area, the policyholders' addresses were collected from the respective branches and were contacted at their work places or residences. In the rural area, the policyholders were contacted at the branch, and those who had a recent service experience and willing to respond, only were interviewed personally. In all, 390 policyholders responded to the questionnaire:

Conventional Branch: n=102, Career-Agents Branch: n= 95, SSS Branch: n= 90, Rural Branch: n=103. Total = 390.

Necessary care was taken to ensure that the sufficient number of respondents covering all the groups of age, income, occupation, education, insurance experience, etc. were included in the sample.

Respondents' Profile

The profile of the respondents shows that they are multi-disciplinary with different socio-economic background. Most of them are male policyholders, in the age of group of 26 to 55years, and literate with secondary school to professional education. They are from various occupational classes (workers, clerical, officers, professional, and business people) with their monthly income ranging from less than Rs.2500 to Rs.15000 or more. All respondents are having more than one-year experience with LIC and nearly 50% are with more than 10 years of experience. (Profile are given in Appendix-III)

Data Analysis

The responses from the respondents were codified and entered in FoxPro. The preliminary analysis of the responses was done using frequency distribution and two-way tables. The relationships between certain variables were studied using Pearson Correlation Coefficients, while the impacts of the variables on the others were measured through linear regressions and logistic regressions. The multivariate analysis was performed using Factor Analysis. The necessary tables and descriptive statistics such as Mean, Standard Deviations, etc. were generated by using Microsoft Excel software package. For certain analyses wherever the application of advanced statistics i.e. Factor analysis, Regression, Logistic regression, etc., were felt necessary, the same were carried-out using the advanced statistical packages namely SAS & SPSS. (A brief note about the statistical test used in the study is given in Appendix-iv) The validity and reliability of the data were tested: construct validity was examined by using factor analysis and reliability of the data was tested by using Cronbach's Coefficient alpha. (The details of all these analyses are given in the respective chapters). The interactions held with the groups representing servicing staff, agents, and executives of LIC, and the documented observations of the researcher were properly analyzed. Similarly, the suggestions received from policyholders, servicing staff, agents, and executives of LIC, were also analyzed in order to identify commonalties and inconsistencies, if any. The important suggestions were incorporated in the final chapter for the consideration of the concerned authorities.

Scope of the study

This study can enable LIC to know customer satisfactions of the service quality parameters: Agents services - pre-sale as well as after-sale services, Products, and Office services. Besides, the study identified the factors determining the satisfaction of these parameters. This would also help understand the deficiencies in service quality and make suitable changes to overcome the same.

It would help the Corporation to know the actual performance at its operating offices in the context of customers' perceived service quality, and locating the stages where the quality is dissatisfactory in the process of the service delivery and the reasons thereof. This can improve the efficiency of the service performance of the operating offices of LIC.

A conceptual model for assessing the service quality is developed. This would help to know the linear relationship among the service quality parameters and the impact of each on the subsequent services, which can also help prioritizing the improvement of these parameters.

The Service Quality Index has been developed to measure the service quality in the operating offices of LIC, which can be general enough to be comparable, and benchmark across it's various offices. This can also be used to monitor the customer's satisfaction easily and speedily.

This model indicates on what dimensions or factors, the service quality is being evaluated by the customers, so that the Corporation can concentrate on those dimensions to render the services satisfactorily.

The study measures the impact of customer satisfaction on Life Insurance business, which helps the management to know the significance of customer satisfaction and to identify loyal customers, volume of repeat business, corporate image and word of mouth effects.

'Perceptual - maps' for each of the selected branches are also developed in this study which could help the management to know how the customers perceive it's performances against the important dimensions.

As the literature on service quality is scanty, this study throws light on new dimensions to service quality.

Limitations of the study

In this study, the assessment of service quality in LIC has been limited to only three urban branches of Pune Division in Maharashtra, and one rural branch of Madurai Division in Tamil Nadu, while LIC has a very wide net-work of operating offices spread all over India. Hence, the findings of the study pertain only to the selected branches. However, the theory and model developed in this study is universal and can be adapted to any branch office with the relevant data.

This study has been done with the limited financial budget, and, therefore, the collection of data was restricted to two Divisions only.

In this study, the impact of satisfaction on life insurance business has been measured under semi-competitive market conditions. However, a similar study can also be done in monopolistic and high competitive market conditions.

In this study, service quality has been measured by customers' perceptions. Obtaining the perceptions of Contact-Service people, Marketing people, and the Management can reveal possibly the other side of service quality.

Review of literature

A brief note about the studies which have served a main base for the present study are given below:

The pioneering work was done by A. Parasuraman, Leonard L. Berry, and Valerie Zeithaml, beginning 1985, who wrote many papers on this subject besides a monograph in 1990, and a series of books on the same theme. They identified ten dimensions of the service quality that may relate to any service: tangibles, reliability, responsiveness, competence, access, courtesy, communication, credibility, security, and understanding the customer[10]. Later in1988, these ten dimensions were combined into five: tangibles, reliability, responsiveness, assurance, and empathy. They measured the service quality using the above ten dimensions in four different service industries: retail banking, credit card, securities brokerage, and product repair and maintenance. Here, the service quality has been measured through customers perceived service quality as the discrepancy or gap between their perceptions and expectations.

While Crosby(1984)[11] defined quality as 'conformance to requirements', Juran (1988)[12] considered this as 'fitness for use'. Evert Gummesson and Gronroos (1989)[13] postulated the quality as a holistic concept, and developed an integrated quality approach by combining the two models of quality: one based on the study of service sector and the other one on the industry sector (Manufacturing). Holistic quality recognizes that all organisations produce and sell both goods and services but in varying proportions and that the customer is buying the utility and need satisfaction, not goods or services as such. U.S. Department of Commerce (1993)[14] developed 'Malcolm Baldridge award' - the core value of the U.S. trophy for outstanding quality, based on customer-driven quality. The award criteria states: 'Quality is judged by the customer. All product and service attributes that contribute value to the customer and lead to customer satisfaction and preference must be the foundation of a company's value system'.

Kenneth Teas (1993)[15] suggested that 'over-all satisfaction should be measured as a transaction to be a function of customers' assessment of service quality, product quality, and price'; and applying this concept is a good area for further research. J. Joseph Cronin, Jr. and Steven A.Taylor (1992)[16] developed a measure called 'SERVPERF' to assess service quality in service industries. They concluded that their measure (SERVPERF) is superior to the SERVQUAL measure developed by A. Parasuraman et al. (1985) on the contention that 'Perception-Expectation dis-confirmation paradigm' used in the SERVQUAL, is a double counting as perception itself is a result of comparison between Expectation and the Actual experience, hence, deducting expectation score from the perception score makes it a double counting. Further, they said 'service quality is an attitude purely based on the service performance.

Anita Van De Vliet (1997)[17] states, 'whatever the methods of measurement used - surveys, focus groups, individual relationships, bench marking, etc. - there are two distinct objectives: on the one hand, you are trying to discover how important particular issues (queuing line, delivery schedules, price, staff friendliness, etc.,) are to your customers, and on the other hand, you need to know how well your company is doing in these critical areas, to track performances over time and to measure improvements'. She further says, "Quadrant analysis with 'How important?' and 'How well are we doing?" as the two axes, can be extremely revealing'. Similarly, Cronin J. Joseph, and others. (1994)[18] suggested that, 'Developing performance-important maps using SERVPERF scale is one currently unexplored areas'.

The review of these studies helps to conclude that quality is a holistic concept, all characteristics of products and services together determine quality. Quality does not result from the output only as services evolve in interaction with the customers; all factors become important determinants. They also suggest that quality lies in customer's perception and it should be measured using all the important factors as perceived by them.

Claes Fornell (1992)[19] developed an annual Customer Satisfaction Barometer (CSB) to measure the customer satisfaction in more than 30 industries and 100 corporations, which measures quality of output (as experienced by the customers). It is a weighted composite index based on 30 industries and 100 corporations, used to evaluate the economy as a whole. This index is specified as a composite latent variable in a system represented by multiple equations, where measurement error is accounted for. Similarly, Eugene. W. Anderson, Claes Fornell, and Michael D. Johnson, Jaesung Cha, & B.E. Bryant (1995)[20] developed an American Customer Satisfaction Index (ACSI) using a set of customer-based performance measures that can be matched to economic performance measures, such as market share and Return on Investment (ROI). ACSI uses a multiple indicator approach to measure an overall customer satisfaction as a latent variable. This index was calculated by combining the facets of customer satisfaction into a single index by using unit weighting schemes or some variation of factor analysis. Further, this index was constructed using a methodology that maximizes the relationship between customer satisfaction and the likelihood of repeat purchase. These suggest a need for developing a weighted composite index to measure the service quality through latent variable approach using multiple measures in an equation.

A. Parasuraman et al. (1996)[21] studied the relationship of service quality on customers' behavioral responses. Their study had shown a strong empirical evidence that service quality has a significant impact on the customers' behavioral responses. Similarly, Ronald T. Rust, Anthony J. Zahorik, and Timothy L. Keiningham (1995)[22] studied the impact of service quality on market share, and concluded that 'quality is an investment, and Return on Quality can be calculated which can make the service quality financially accountable'. Vikas Mittal, William T. Ross, Jr., and Patrick M. Baldasane (1998)[23] concluded that over-all satisfaction or service quality is a multi-attribute construct, and the relationship between attribute-level performance, over-all satisfaction, and repurchase intention is of critical importance and they have been conceptualized as linear and symmetric. Their result showed that negative performance on an attribute has a greater impact on over-all satisfaction and repurchases intention than the positive performance.

To sum up, these studies have stressed a need for measuring the effect of service quality on customers' behavioral responses. However, such studies already conducted on service quality may be found inadequate in insurance industry. To elaborate, studies conducted, thusfar, have mainly focused on measuring the service quality through some selected parameters only. In particular, in Life Insurance, no study has been done for measuring service quality in totality, and it's impact on Life Insurance business. In India also, no such studies have been done so far. Finally, there is an absence of well-established index available to measure the perceived service quality in totality, and the existing studies are also silent in this regard. Therefore, the present study is undertaken to fill up the gap in the literature regarding the vital aspects of the service quality in insurance industry.

REFERENCES

1. Claes Fornell, Michael D. Johnson, Eugene W. Anderson, Jaesung Cha, and Barbara Everitt Bryant (1996), "The American Customer Satisfaction Index: Nature, Purpose, and Findings," Journal of Marketing, 60 (October), P. 11.
2. 'Vision 2001: Service Management and Image Building' (1997), GIC, Mumbai, P. 1.
3. Anderson, Eugene W., Claes Fornell, and Donald R. Lehmann (1994), "Customer Satisfaction, Market Share, and Profitability," Journal of Marketing, 58 (July), P. 55.
4. Parasuraman A., Valarie A. Zeithaml, and Leonard Berry (1985), "A Conceptual Model of Service Quality and its Implications for Further Research," Journal of Marketing, 48 (Fall), P. 41-50.
5. Ibid, P. 41-43.
6. Ibid, P. 41-43.
7. Ibid, P. 41-43.
8. Ibid, P. 41-43.
9. Ibid, P. 41-43.
10. Ibid, P. 41-43.
11. Philip Crosby (1993), Quality is Free, New York: McGraw Hill, Inc.
12. Gummesson E. (1991), "Service Quality - A Holistic View," in Service Quality: Multidisciplinary and Multinational Perspectives, Brown S.W., Gummesson E., Edvardsson E., and Gustavsson B. (eds.), Lexington, MA: Lexington Books, P. 3.
13. Ibid, P. 17.
14. Richard T. Watson (1998), "Measuring Information Systems Service Quality: Lessons From Two Longitudinal Case Studies," Management of Information Science Quarterly, (March), P. 61.

15. Teas, R. Kenneth (1993), "Expectations, Performance Evaluation, and Consumer Perceptions of Quality," Journal of Marketing, 57 (October), P. 18-34.

16. Cronin J.Joseph, Jr., and Steven A. Taylor (1992), "Measuring Service Quality: A Re-examination and Extension," Journal of Marketing, 56 (July), P. 55-68.

17. Anita Van de Vliet (1997), "Best Practice - Are they being served?," Management Today, (February) P. 66-72.

18. Cronin J. Joseph, Jr., and Steven A. Taylor (1994), "SERVPERF Versus SERVQUAL: Reconciling Performance-Based and Perceptions-Minus- Expectations Measurement of Service Quality," Journal of Marketing, 58 (January), P. 130.

19. Claes Fornell (1992), "A National Customer Satisfaction Barometer: The Swedish Experience," Journal of Marketing, 55 (January), P. 1-21.

20. Claes Fornell, Michael D. Johnson, Eugene W. Anderson, Jaesung Cha, and Barbara Everitt Bryant (1996), "The American Customer Satisfaction Index: Nature, Purpose, and Findings," Journal of Marketing, 60 (October), P. 7-18.

21. Valarie A. Zeithaml, Leonard L. Berry, and Parasuraman A. (1996), "The Behavioral Consequences of Service Quality," Journal of Marketing, 60 (April), P. 31-46.

22. Roland T. Rust, Anthony J. Zahorik, and L. Keiningham (1995), "Return on Quality (ROQ): Making Service Quality Financially Accountable," Journal of Marketing, 59 (April), P. 58-70.

23. Vikas Mittal, William T.Ross, Jr., and Patrick M. Houston (1998), "The Asymmetric Impact of Negative and Positive Attribute-Level Performance on Over-all Satisfaction and Repurchase Intentions," Journal of Marketing, 62 (January), P. 33-47.

Chapter 3

TOTAL QUALITY ASSESSMENT

Introduction

This chapter makes references to various definitions of quality to have better understanding of the term, and provides a relevant definition for 'total quality in life insurance'. It also discusses about the methods of quality measurement and importance of total quality assessment in life insurance through customers' perceptions.

Definitions of Quality

The term "Quality' is referred as Goodness of a Product or Service, Durability, Reliability, Defect Free, etc. The Oxford dictionary defines quality as *'The degree of excellenece of a thing'*. Juran[1] defines quality as *'meeting of specification of a product'* (i.e.) in automobiles, exact measurement of engine capacity (300 c.c.), fuel consumption (80 kpl) are the specifications, and quality results when the product meets these specifications. "A good piece of craftsmanship (an artistic product) is also considered as quality.

These definitions are product based, and not exhaustive in the sense that they do not cover all aspects of service quality. In these, some selected factors such as durability, aesthetic value, reliability,

performance, features, etc., are considered as quality indicators, and mere existence of such factors in the finished product is perceived as quality. But, quality relies not only on final outcome of service or finished product, but also on experience that one undergoes during the process of production of a service.

A. Parasuraman, Valarie A.Zeithaml, and Leonard L.Berry[2] say 'Production and Consumption of many services are one and the same. So, quality occurs during the service delivery, usually in an interaction between the client and contact person from the service firm. Quality evaluations are not made solely on die outcome of a service; they also involve evaluations of the process of the service delivery'. Gronroos (1983)[3] postulated that two types of service quality exist: Technical quality that involves what the customer is actually receiving from the service, and functional quality, which refers to the manner in which the service is delivered. Lehtinen and Lehtinen (1982)[4] confirmed that service quality occurs through the interaction between customer and elements in the service organization (Physical elements: place, building, equipment; personnel; corporate quality - company image or profile); and interactive quality between contact person and customer, or customer and another customer. Evert Gummessan[5] says 'Quality is not just the output of a rational, logical and impersonal productive system. As service evolves in interaction with customers' empathy, a caring personality, desire to serve, emotions, involvement, compassion, sense of humor, facet of knowledge and intuition - all dimensions of the love factor - become essential, even the decisive contributors to service quality'. Garvin (1987)[6] defines Quality as the characteristics of the following: Function, Features, Conformance, Reliability, Serviceability, Aesthetics, company image. Easy accessibility. Providing prompt attention. Offering expertise. Providing the leading technology, and Providing for cost effectiveness. The above definitions and views contribute that service quality does not result merely from functional quality, it depends on various factors such as physical appearance of office, machines, people, writing materials, facilities available to the customers, knowledge and competence of the office people, responsiveness to the customers' needs, time taken for performing the service, reliability, empathy, etc.,

User based quality definitions;

Philip Crospy[7] defines quality' as 'conformance to requirements' Here, the requirements refer to consumer's requirements. He states that, if a product conforms to the requirements of consumers, it achieves quality.

Again, Juran defines it as 'fitness for use' *i.e.* if a product fulfills the primary purpose or the requirements for which it was brought.

Quality is 'High Performance' for the users of products or services. The consumers expect a maximum performance (superior) from the products or services that they purchased. Similarly, the sales people expect that the products or services that they sell should give maximum performance to the customers.

Crosby defines it as 'Zero Defects' emphasizing the products or services should be defect free. This provides high value - for the users whose work is disturbed by those defects and for the quality control \ assurance manager whose main goal is ensuring defects free products or services. Quality is 'User Friendliness.' It means high value - for those who have a very high involvement with the product or services (users of computer or software), whose transactions are highly personalised or requires more intimacy.

Quality has been associated with 'lots of features'. This gives high value for the marketers who believe .those features sell products, similarly, for the customers who demand more value for the price.

Total Quality - Concepts

The International Standard Organisation (ISO)[8] defines quality as 'The totality of features and characteristics of a product or service that bear on its ability to satisfy stated and implied needs'. 'The totality of features and characteristics of a product or service' indicates that quality results not from a particular feature of service or product, but it relies on total offerings of all features, 'ability to satisfy ....needs' indicates a customer oriented attitude; 'stated or implied needs' indicates that customers sometimes can and sometimes cannot articulate their needs and that the suppliers must actively attempt to make their own interpretations and continuously improve their understanding of the customer. Based on this definition, the present study presents a new definition for the term "Total Quality' as "Totality of all features and characteristics of products, services, systems, and people that gives complete satisfaction."This definition emphasize total quality of all the Components or aspects involved in delivering complete satisfaction to the users. It encompasses all the features of products, characteristics of the multi-dimensional aspects of services, systems and the processes, and the people involved in the production of quality. Quality is a multi-dimensional attributes - it ensures absolute perfection, zero defects, high performance, more value, complete satisfaction, systems or process improvements, people development, etc.

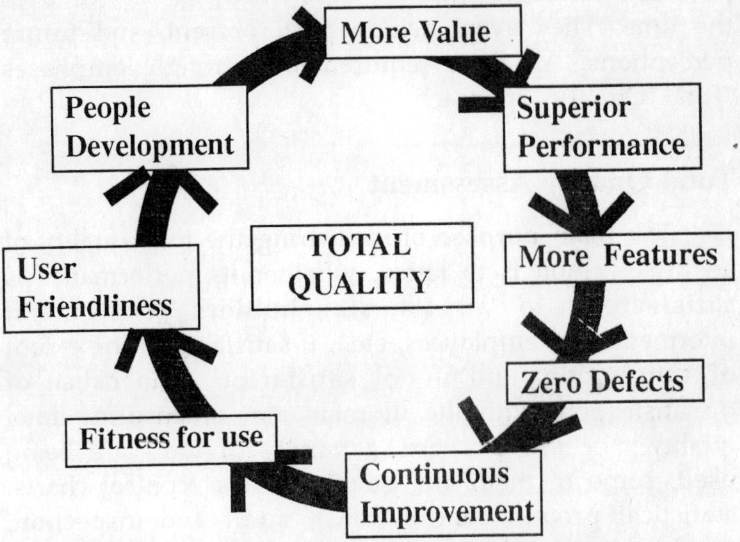

It has been noted that quality requirements are different from business to business, customer to customer, suppliers, dealers, technical people, servicing people, and the other stakeholders. Quality ensures meeting the needs or requirements of all the people associated with quality. This emphasis that the organisations working for 'quality' needs to have 'Total Quality' approach to ensure complete satisfaction to all the people associated with the organisation. Secondly, the organization should have quality support structure. This means, all the components of the organizational structure - the various hierarchical networks (Zones, Divisions, Branches, etc.). Departments (Production, Marketing, Planning, Finance, etc.), and the systems and processes, should support delivering quality. In addition, it demands for commitment to quality from the people at all the levels. Quality perceptions are the attitudes based on overall judgment. They .do not result from the mere individual transaction specific purchases (specific service occasion), they do depend on the total purchase and consumption experiences of service over the time. They even include past, present, and future perceptions. All these requirements strongly emphases 'Total Quality' approach.

Total Quality Assessment

The main purpose of measuring the total quality of an organisation is to know, whether its performance is satisfactory to all its stakeholders (customers, intermediaries, employees, etc.), if satisfactory, the extent of satisfaction; and if not satisfactory, the cause of dissatisfaction; with the ultimate aim of ensuring total quality. For this purpose, a variety of tools are being used, some of them are: quality circles, 'control charts, statistical process control (SPC), audit and inspection, etc. In this regard, standards are set internally and, the quality is measured by comparing the actual performance with them. When the quality is measured through the quality circle or audit and inspection, it becomes an internal evaluation, and the service performance of an office may be found good according to such internal evaluation, but the same performance may be perceived as poor by the customers due to a gap between the internal standards and customers' expectations. And, the parameters that the customers' use for evaluating the service performance may be different from those used in the internal evaluation. Moreover, only quantitative aspects are measured, and the qualitative aspects are not taken into account. But in the customer-based measurement, these aspects form part of the measurement itself.

So, the customer-based measurement is considered as the best method for assessing total service quality. The customer is the best judge of quality of service, superior quality is there, if he says so, and the only true and reliable measurement of total quality would be the assessment of customer's experiences with the organisation, and his level of satisfaction with those experiences. Tom Peter with Nancy Austin[9] in their book: A Passion for excellence says, 'Service, its substance, quality and value, lies solely in the mind and hearts of customers -, as they perceive it. An organisation can provide the best service possible, but if customers do not accept it as the best, it is not. There is only a perceived reality, the way each of us chooses to perceive a communication, the value of a service, the value of a particular product feature, and quality of a product - the real is what we perceive, and the feelings are facts. The individual perceives service in his or her own terms'. Moreover, since quality is an attitude, measuring through customer's perception becomes an appropriate evaluation.

Further, it is important to note that the emerging literature largely supports the perception-based measurement. Parasuraman, Zeithaml, and Berry (1985)[10] conclude in their research report that service quality judgements comprise five underlying attributes that consumers evaluate as the basis of the expectancy-disconfirmation Paradigm. Cronin and Taylor (1992)[11] say that 'Service Quality is directly influenced only by perception (of performance)'. Other recent studies also come out with the similar conclusions; Bolton and Drew (1991), Peter Churchill and Brown (1992), and Babakus and Boiller (1992), and Babakus and Mangold (1992) support the use of performance- based measures of service quality[12] Further, J.Joseph Cronin, Jr., and Steven A. taylor (1994)[13] suggest that 'performance-based measurement of service quality is better method over others'. Therefore, in this study, *service quality is measured by customer's perception.*

Total Quality Assessment in Life Insurance

In life insurance, from the stage of buying a product to final consumption of service (claim settlement) the perception of service quality is affected by a number of factors such as product features, agent's services, office services, etc. When the service quality of an organisation is assessed through customers' perceptions, it is necessary to evaluate all the possible factors affecting their perceptions.

A thorough analysis of the conceptual definitions of service quality, and discussions with the customers, agents, contract service people, departmental heads, and the management have helped to define the total quality in life insurance as 'Totality of all features and characteristics of products, services, systems, and people that gives complete satisfaction.' Here, product means the life insurance policy that the customer has; services refer to - all the pre-sale and after-sale services of agents, and offices; systems relates to all the systems and processes involved in delivering quality, and people refer to - service people who render the service, and all others who are associated with quality.

This definition suggests that service quality needs to be measured in term's of 1. Product, 2.Agent's service, and 3.Office service. Insurance service can be looked at 'three sides': Product, Agents, and the Company.

The Insurance Services Traiangle

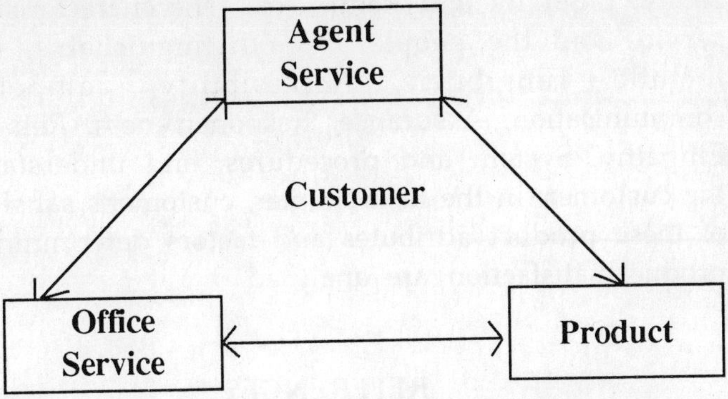

The three sides of the triangle represent service delivery. If service quality is not being adequately provided by any of the service lines, the client in the middle gets squeezed. If one side of the triangle decides to expand the service delivery without a co-ordinated and corresponding service extension with the other arms, the triangle becomes lopsided and loses its balance. Maintaining these new service levels becomes increasingly difficult. In this study, the service quality is measured using an index (the details about the index and the results are given in chapter-7). The above three parameters are also the parameters of the index. The measurement of these three parameters, and the significant factors driving these measures are dealt in the subsequent chapters.

Summary

The analysis of the various service quality concepts as defined in various studies (Reference 1-13) and the assessment methods, have helped to define 'total quality' in life insurance as Totality of all features and characteristics of products, services, systems, and people that gives complete satisfaction'. In life insurance, the product features are risk protection, Savings, Tax benefits, Safety, Liquidity and Return, etc. The characteristics of service and the people are indistinguishable, which include Tangibility, Accessibility, competence, communication, Assurance, Responsiveness, Reliability, Empathy, System and procedures, and understanding the customer. In the next chapter, customer's satisfaction of these product attributes and factors determining the product satisfaction are analysed.

REFERENCES

1 J.M. Juran (1988), Planning for Quality, New York: The Free Press, P. 5.

2 Parasuraman A., Valarie A. Zeithaml, and Leonard Berry (1985), "A Conceptual Model of Service Quality and its Implications for Further Research," Journal of Marketing, 48 (Fall), P. 41 -50.

3 'Quality Management in Service Organisations' (1993), by Evert Gummesson, ISQA, Sweden, P. 222.

4 Parasuraman A., et al., (1985), P. 41-50.

5 Gummesson E. (1991), "Service Quality - A Holistic View," in Service *Quality: Multidisciplinary and Multinational Perspectives,* Brown S.W., Gummesson E., Edvardsson E,, and Gustavsson B. (eds.), Lexington, MA: Lexington Books, P. 3.

6 David A. Garvin (1987), 'Competing on the eight dimensions of quality," Harvard Business Review, (November-December), P. 104-108.

7. "Philip Crosby (1993), Quality is Free, New York: McGraw Hill, Inc.

8 Dennis Green (1996), The complete ISO 9000 Manual, London: Kogan Page Ltd., P. 13.

9 Tom Peters and Nancy Austin (1986), A Passion for Excellence, New York: Warner Books, P. 83.

10 Parasuraman A., et al. (1985), P. 41-50.

11 Cronin J.Joseph, Jr., and Steven A. Taylor (1992), "Measuring Service Quality: A Re-examination and Extension," Journal of Marketing, 56 (July), P. 58.

12 Cronin J. Joseph(1994), P. 126.

13 Cronin J. Joseph, Jr., and Steven A. Taylor (1994), "SERVPERF Versus SERVQUAL : Reconciling Performance-Based and Perceptions-Minus- Expectations Measurement of Service Quality," *Journal of Marketing*, 58 (January), P. 126-127.

Chapter 4

PRODUCT SATISFACTION AND MEASUREMENT

Introduction

This chapter focuses mainly on: i) measuring the Product Satisfaction through customer's perception, and ii) identifying the factors determining product satisfaction.

Product Satisfaction, refer to "policyholders' satisfactions with their LIC policy(ies)". In India, Life Insurance policies are mostly bought for multiple needs, i.e. for risk protection, savings, tax benefits, etc. Customer's satisfaction with the policies may thus be said to depend on how the product satisfies these needs. Again, the market itself is driven by the concept of value for money, hence, while evaluating the product satisfaction, customer perception of the cost of product will also have to be considered as an important variable. Thirdly, savings being one of the important reasons for buying life insurance, the rate of return on them may also play a vital role in determining the product satisfaction. Similarly, liquidity and safety being the other important investment parameters, while evaluating the life insurance products, they have to be taken into account. Thus, these factors serve as a basis for the measurement.

Measurement of product satisfaction

Product satisfaction was measured as an over-all composite measure of need satisfaction, cost, return, liquidity and safety of the product:

Product Satisfaction='Function of need satisfaction+ cost of product+rate of return+liquidity+safety of product'.

Here, need satisfaction specifically refers to the macro needs for life insurance policies i.e. risk protection, savings, tax benefits, retirement benefits, children's education and marriage, etc. Cost of the product means 'the amount of premium that the policy holders pay for their policies'.

Product satisfaction score was obtained by averaging the scores of these variables* together (Before averaging, the scores of all the variables were standardised since the scale value of some of the variables (i.e.) need satisfaction, and cost, are not uniform).

Customer satisfaction of life insurance policies

The analysis reveals that the *over-all product satisfactions of majority* (74%) of the customers are 'moderate'. Only a small percentage of them (15%) are satisfied with the policies, while 11% are dissatisfied. This moderate satisfaction with the life insurance policies could be mainly due to very large number of policyholders being not satisfied with the return and liquidity aspects of the LIC policies (Ref: Table 4.1 & Figure 4.1).

Table 4.1
Customer Satisfaction of LIC policies:

Satisfaction	No	%
Poor	40	11%
Moderate	266	74%
Good	54	15%
Grand Total	360	100%

Figure 4.1
Product Satisfaction

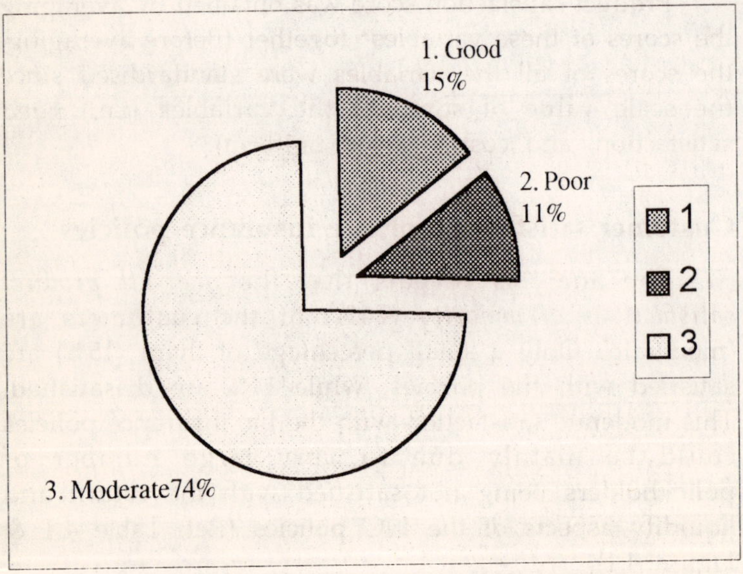

In order to know which aspects of the product satisfaction need further improvement, the customers' perceptions of each variable constituting the product satisfaction i.e., need satisfaction, cost of the product, return, etc., were obtained. The findings are given below:

- A high percentage (95%) of policyholders are satisfied with their policies in meeting their primary needs i.e., risk protection, savings, and tax benefits etc., (Mean = 1.91, & S.D = 0.28). (Ref: Table 4.2)

Table 4.2

Customer's perception of LIC's policies in satisfying their needs:

Perceptions	No	%
Satisfied	31	5%
Dissatisfied	327	95%
Total	358	100%

- As many as 74% of the policyholders have perceived the premium of their policies as *'reasonable'*, and 22% as 'high'. A very low percentage (4%) of people felt it as 'low' (Mean = 1.77 & S.D = 0.42) (Ref: Table 4.3).

Table 4.3

Customer's perception about Premium:

Satisfaction	No	%
High	83	22%
Reasonable	279	74%
Low	15	4%
Grand Total	377	100%

- 37% policyholders are *satisfied* with the return of their policies. While 31% of them perceive it as 'poor', the remaining (32%) have felt as 'moderate' (Mean = 3.02 & S.D = 0.94). The perception of return on the LIC polices is *'poor'* in comparison with other financial products such as Bank Deposits, UTI, PPF, NSC, and Postal savings (Ref: Table 4.4, & Figure 4.2).

Table 4.4
Customer's perception about Returns on the LIC's policies.

Satisfaction	No	%
Poor	98	30%
Moderate	104	32%
Good	120	37%
Grand Total	322	100%

Figure 4.2
LIC's Return in comparision to other Financial Products

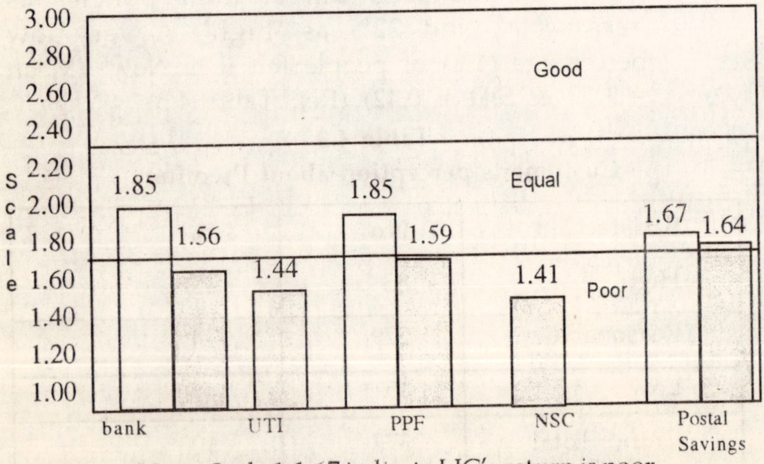

Note : Scale 1-1-67 indicate LIC's return is poor

- The liquidity of the LIC policies has been perceived as *'poor'* in comparison with Bank Deposits, UTI, PPF, NSC, and Postal savings (Ref: Figure 4.4).

Figure 4.4
LIC's Liquidity in comparision to other financial products

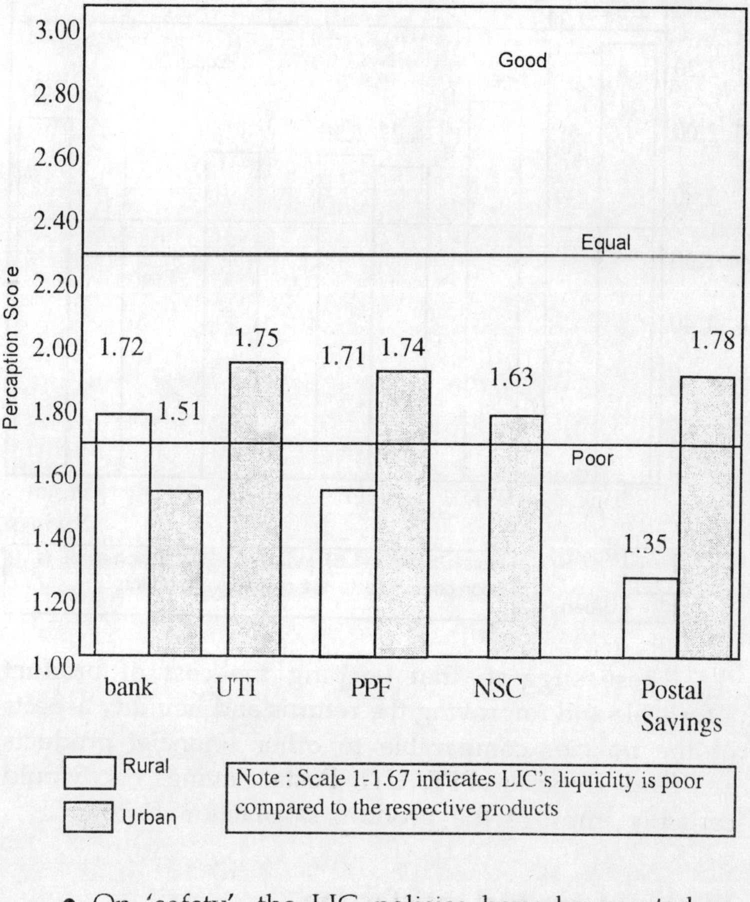

- On 'safety', the LIC policies have been rated as *'equal'* in comparison with Bank Deposits, UTI, PPF, NSC, and Postal savings (Ref: Figure 4.3).

Figure 4.3

LIC's Safety in comparision to other financial products

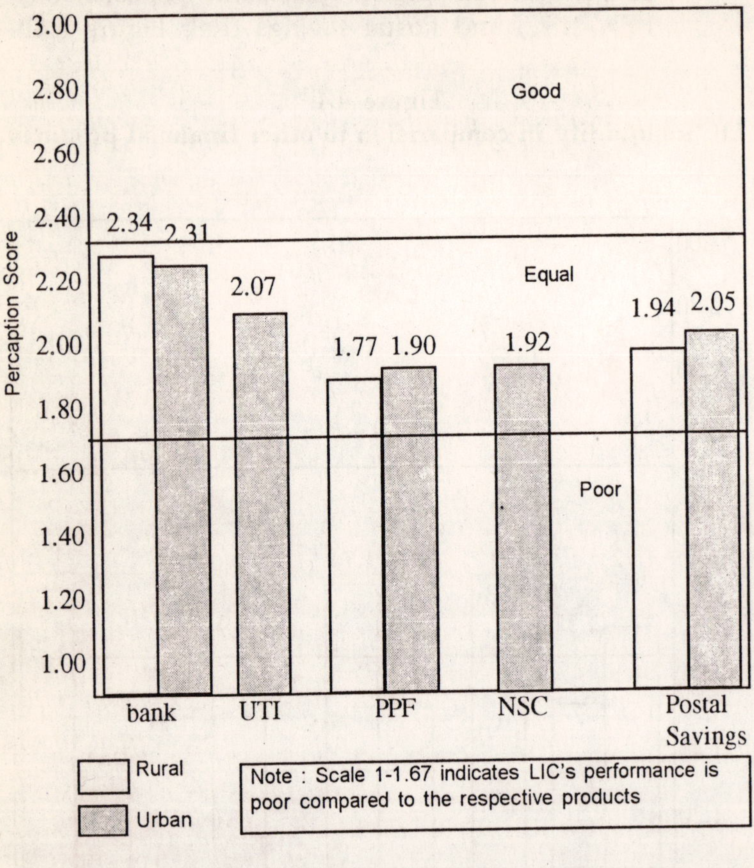

These suggest, that keeping the cost of product affordable and improving the returns and liquidity aspects of the policies comparable to other financial products i.e., Bank Deposits, PPF, UTI, Postal Savings etc., would certainly improve the product satisfaction further.

Factors of product satisfaction

As Life Insurance policies are generally bought for combination of various needs i.e., risk protection, savings, tax benefits etc., the number of variables affecting the product satisfaction would be many. Secondly, since life insurance product itself is latent in nature, the factors affecting product satisfaction might be latent factors rather than individual variables. This may cause some difficulty in knowing which variables are the important factors of product satisfaction. If, through some statistically reliable methods, the important factors and their extent of influence on product satisfaction, are identified, it would help for effective product positioning and also for developing customer driven product-mix. For this purpose, the following variables are selected:

1. *Risk Protection:* Risk protection is the core benefit of life insurance that distinguishes life insurance from financial products. As it is expected to be one of the main factors to buy life insurance policies, it has been assumed to have a greater impact on product satisfaction.

2. *Savings:* Life insurance is perceived more as a financial product rather than risk cover. This factor may also play a significant role in affecting the satisfaction.

3. *Tax Benefits:* The availability of certain tax benefits on the investment in life policies mostly serves as one of the prime motives for buying the policies. But, whether the tax benefits alone determine the product satisfaction needs to be tested since there are a quite few other products also having tax benefits.

4. *Need Satisfaction:* The importance of this variable has already been discussed in the introduction.

5. *Cost:* This variable has also been discussed in the same para (2) of this chapter.

6. *Return:* It has been observed that life insurance policies are sold mostly as savings instruments with an assurance of a steady rate of return during the entire

term of the policy. Customers' perceptions on return on this investment in comparison with the other financial products would also affect the product satisfaction.

7. *Liquidity:* Since life insurance policies are generally long term contracts, how the customers perceive the liquidity in comparison with the other long term products i.e. Public Provident Fund, National Saving Certificate, Unit Trust Of India, etc., may also be the significant factor.

8. *Safety:* Safety is one of the main parameters being used while evaluating the financial products. Many of these products are today subjected to certain norms and regulations of the Reserve Bank Of India and Stock Exchange Bureau of India (SEBI), besides the Credit Ratings by CRISIL, ICRA, CARE, etc. Hence, how LIC policies are perceived in comparison with the other financial products in terms of safety may also have an impact on the satisfaction.

9. *Agent's Pre-Sales service:* The knowledge about life insurance products is limited among the policyholders, so, the agents render certain pre-sales services like explaining policy benefits, cost, mode of payment, selection of policy, etc., to their customers. Therefore, the quality of these pre-sales services would also affect the satisfaction.

10. *After-sale services of Agents, and 11. Services of operating offices:* Life insurance is a latent product and its benefits are received only either at the time of maturity of policies or on the occurrence of certain contingency (Death). The quality of various after-sales services that the customers experience either at the branch office or from their agents, is, therefore, expected to have significant impact on product satisfaction.

The description of all the variables used for the analysis is given below:

Table 4.5
Description of the variables

Variables	Description of data
1. Risk	Reasons for the purchase (1=least important to 4=most important).
2. Savings	-do-
3. Tax	-do-
4. Need Satisfaction	Numerical ratings: where 1= dissatisfied, 2 = satisfied.
5. Cost	Numerical ratings: where 1= high, 2 = moderate, 3 = low
6. Return[1]	Average value of LIC in comparison to Bank Deposits, UTI, PPF, NSC, and Postal Savings.
7. Safety*[1]	-do- -do-
8. Liquidity*[1]	-do- -do-
9. Pre-sales service[2]	Average value of pre-sale service items.
10. After-sales service[3]	Average value of after-sale service items.
11. SERVPERF[4]	Average value of office service items.

Latent factors determining the product satisfaction

Initially, under the assumption that the above selected variables would be interrelated with each other, a correlation matrix of these variables was obtained. The correlation matrix revealed a moderate level of inter-correlation among the variables. The inter-relationship has suggested that these variables are multivariate in nature and influence product satisfaction in combination of two or more variables rather than individually. Moreover, these variables were assumed to be the linear combinations of some underlying (latent) factors, which account for such inter-relationship among them. Probably, these latent factors may be the determinants of product satisfaction rather than the individual variables. This assumption has led to use factor analysis[5] to identify the underlying factors accounting for product satisfaction. Further, it can also help in identifying the most significant factors of product satisfaction. For this purpose, Factor analysis was carried out on the 11 selected variables, which were assumed to be the influencing factors of product satisfaction. Principle Component Analysis[6] has been used as a method for obtaining the initial factors. The principle component analysis extracted four factors with the eigen values[7] of 2.89, 1.52, 1.30, and 1.01 (Kaiser's criteria of eigen values greater than 1 has been used as a base for selecting the factors). These four factors together explain 61% variation.

Examination of the factor matrix given by the principal component analysis suggested that the factor structure is not clear and the factors are inter-correlated. Hence in order to get the clear factor structure interpretable in terms of the associated variables, the four factors obtained through the principle component analysis were rotated for oblique rotation using 'Direct Oblimine'[8] method. The factor loading of each variable in the respective factor can be interpreted as the correlation of the variable with the factor; high factor loading represents high correlation. The rotated structure matrix gives a very clear structure of the factor loading. (Ref: Figure 4.6).

Table 4.6
Structure Matrix

Variables	Factor 1	Factor 2	Factor 3	Factor4
SAVINGS	.72*	.05	.32	-.37
RISK	-.19	-.08	-.01	.87*
TAX	-.66*	.001	-.22	.10
RETURN	.30	.71*	.04	.15
SAFETY	.19	.75*	.09	-.07
LIQUIDITY	-.04	.73*	.22	.12
PRESALE	.23	.19	.86*	.07
AFSALE	.17	.10	.91*	-.06
SERVPERF	.59*	.44	.45	-.16
NEED	.49**	.38	.12	.48
COST	.56*	.25	.02	.10
Eigen values	2.89	1.52	1.30	1.01
% of variance				
Extracted.	26	14	12	9
Cumulative % of variance.	26	40	52	61

(Note: 1.Items having a factor loading of 0.50 or above are considered as significantly loaded in a particular factor, and where an item is loaded in more than one factor significantly, that item has been taken into a factor in which it has the greatest loading.*

*2. The item**, since it has a loading nearer to 0.50 to consider significant and conceptually related to factor-1, has been grouped into factor-1.)*

For interpreting the factor loading, a cut-off point at 0.5 has been considered to determine the significant variables for each factor. The negative signs of the factor loading indicate that these variables contribute in a reverse manner to the concerned factors. Interpretation of the factors was made based on the significant loading of the variables. On the basis of the nature of the variables significantly loaded in the respective factors, suitable names were given to the factors: Factor I and II represent 'Product features' and 'Financial features' respectively. Factor III represents 'Agent's service' and Factor IV explains "Risk feature".

The analysis of these factors has generated following results:

Factor I - Product features: This factor is found to be the most important one as it explains 26% for the underlying continuum of product satisfaction. In this factor, the variable 'savings' has the highest loading (.72), followed by servperf (.59), cost (.56), need (.49) and tax (-.66). This shows that savings attribute of the product seems to be the most important feature in the factor. The second important feature is 'Office service' (servperf) which shows that office service is considered as one of the main product attributes and, the quality of service provided by the branch offices plays a significant role in determining product satisfaction. And, the other important attributes are cost of the product and need satisfaction. The variable 'tax benefits' the other important feature of the product, has a high negative loading. This indicates that in the customer's perception, it seems to be different from the other product features.

Factor II - Financial features of the product: This is the next significant factor contributed to the satisfaction as it explains 14% of product satisfaction. In this, all features of a financial product: Return (.71), Safety (.75), and Liquidity (.73) have greater loading. This shows that all these three features are equally important in determining the product satisfaction.

Factor III - Agent's service: is the third important factor, which explains 12%. Variation. The very high loading of both pre-sale service (.86) and after-sale service (.90) indicates that the role of Agents in giving satisfactory service to the customers also contributes significantly to the underlying continuum.

Factor IV - Risk feature: is found as the least important as it explains only 9% variation in product satisfaction. This shows that only a small section of the customers perceive life insurance as a risk cover, and secondly life insurance products are mostly marketed as a financial product by the agents.

The results suggest that, since the first two factors represent the 'savings' features of the products, life insurance should be positioned more as a financial product rather than risk product. As a financial product, a clear preference for safety, liquidity, and return is seen, which suggests the need to have a product mix of all these attributes. Moreover, if the agents also continuously persuade the importance of the savings feature of life insurance, backed by satisfactory service from both agents and the office, would increase the product satisfaction further.

Summary

In this chapter, Product Satisfaction was measured as a composite measure of need satisfaction, cost of product, return, liquidity and safety of the product. The analysis revealed a moderate customer satisfaction with the LIC policies. The analysis of the factors determining the product satisfaction revealed that the product attributes particularly the financial features, as the most important determiner of satisfaction. Secondly, the agent's service also seems to have significant impact. However, the risk feature (the core benefit of life insurance) appears to have a low impact. The next chapter deals with the assessment of agent's service. It also analyses the factors determining the satisfaction of both pre-sales as well as after-sales services of the agents.

REFERENCES

1 To know customer's perception on LIC's return, liquidity and safety, the customers were asked to compare LIC policies with Bank Deposits, UTI, PPF, NSC and Postal Savings, separately, in terms of return, liquidity and safety by using 3-point scale where Poor=1, Equal=2, and Good=3. The average value of these comparisons of return has been taken as LIC's return perception. High score indicates high return. Similarly, perception for liquidity and safety were obtained.

2 Agent's pre-sales service was measured using a five point scale on the following service items: selection of policy, counselling of financial needs, knowledge and competency, explaining the benefits of various policies, friendliness, assistance in filling up the necessary forms, and attentive to the customers.

3 Agent's after-sales service was measured using a five point scale on the following items: reviewing the insurance needs of their clients, assistance in remittance of premium, assistance in premium notice, assistance in policy documents, and assistance in other after-sales services.

4 Servperf is an office service measure, which is measured using a six-point scale on various office service items.

5 A brief notes on factor analysis are given in Appendix II of the Chapter 1.

6 Principle Component Analysis is a method of transforming a given set of observed variables into another set of variables (principle components) which explains the 'total variance' in the observed variables. It serves a base for extracting the initial factors in Factor Analysis.

7 Eigen Value: a mathematical property of a matrix; used in relation to the decomposition of a covariance matrix both as a criterion of determining the number of factors to extract and a measure of variance accounted for by a given dimension.

8 Direct Oblimine is a rotation method used in factor analysis to get a simple and clear factor structure when the factors are correlated.

Chapter 5

AGENT'S SERVICE SATISFACTION AND MEASUREMENT

Introduction

This chapter covers customer satisfaction of agent's service, it's measurement, and identification of factors determining the satisfaction of the agent's service. For this purpose, the services of agents were divided into two parts: i) pre-sales service and ii) after-sales service, since the nature of these services and their impact on other determinants (product satisfaction, office service, etc.,) differ from one to another. For measuring pre-sales and after-sales services, the following 12 items were selected:

- Selection of policy.
- Counselling of financial needs.
- Knowledge and competency.
- Benefits of various policies.
- Friendliness
- Assistance in filling up the necessary forms.
- Attentive to the customers.
- Review of insurance needs.

- Assistance in remittance of premium.
- Assistance in premium notice.
- Assistance in policy documents.
- Assistance in other after-sales services.

Measurement of Pre sales services

For measuring the pre-sales services of agents, the following aspects of their sales activities were selected:

- Selection of policy.
- Counselling of financial needs.
- Knowledge and competence.
- Benefits of various policies.
- Friendliness
- Assistance in filling up the necessary forms.
- Attentive to the customers.

The customers were asked to state their perceptions about the quality of these services rendered by their agents, by using 5 point Likert scale with adjectives of *very poor, poor, somewhat o.k, good, and very good.* Then a scoring pattern of 1 (very poor} to 5 (very good) was followed. Since all these services measure this construct, the overall satisfaction score on this (pre-sales service) was obtained by averaging the scores of these services combined:

Over-all score = *Selection of policy + Financial advice + Product knowledge + Providing policy Details. +Friendliness + Assistance in filling necessary forms + Attentive to customers.* The High score indicates more favourable attitude towards the pre-sales service.

Customer satisfaction of pre-sales service

The results of the study indicate that customer satisfaction of the *pre sales service is 'moderate', as the mean value* is 3.51. The S.D of 0.75 indicates that their perceptions are moderately dispersed. About 57% of the customers felt this service as 'good' and 30 % felt it as 'moderate', and very few (13%) perceived it as 'poor' (Ref: Table 5.1 & Chart 5.1). The analysis further shows

Table 5.1
Customer Satisfaction of Agent's Pre-sales Service:

Satisfaction	No	%
Poor	43	13%
Moderate	102	30%
Good	191	57%
Grand Total	336	100%

Figure 5.1
Customer Satisfaction of Agent's Pre-sales service

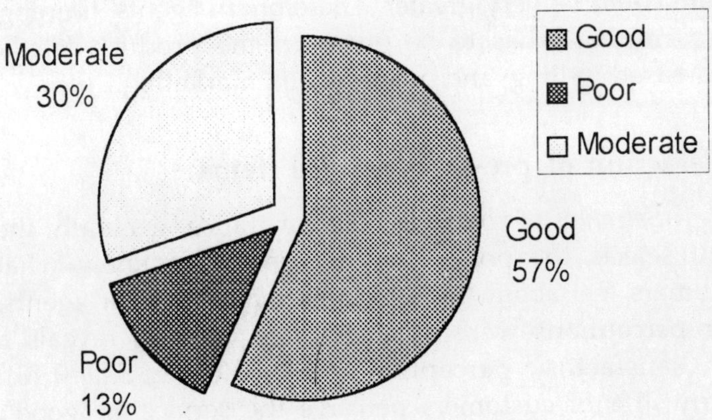

Table 5.1A
Customer Satisfaction and Types of Agents:

Types of agent	Mean value
Ordinary Agents	3.34
Career Agents	3.64
Rural Agents	3.79

that the pre-sales service of rural agents is good (Mean=3.79). This indicates that most of the rural customers feel that their agents have selected appropriate policies after careful analysis of their requirements, and giving them adequate details of the policy. Similarly, the career agent's service has been perceived as good (Mean=3.64), while the ordinary agent's service is found moderate (Mean=3.34) (Ref: Table 5.1A). This further suggests that the ordinary agents in urban areas need to improve their professional knowledge in selling. Since the pre-sales service gives an initial opportunity in developing the customer relationships, and if these services are found dissatisfactory, the impact in terms of loss of future business as well as the negative word of mouth could be very greater. Therefore in agents' training, more emphasis has to be given on the product details, need-based selling and relationship marketing.

Satisfaction of pre-sales service items

1. *Selection of policy:* In Life Insurance, generally the agent selects the policy for his clients. To know what customers feel about the selections made by their agents, their perceptions were obtained. The analysis reveals a high satisfactory perception (Mean=3.67 & S.D=0.78). Nearly 71% of customers perceive the service as 'good', and 21% of them perceived as 'moderate'. Very few

(8%) feel the same as 'poor'. The analysis further reveals that, the services of rural agents were rated as 'good' by a great majority of customers (93%). Similarly, the career agent's service has also received satisfactory perception as nearly 70% of customers felt satisfied, while it is moderate (61%) for ordinary agents (Ref: Table 5.2 & 5.2A).

Table 5.2

Customer Satisfaction of Selection of Policies:

Satisfaction	No	%
Poor	27	8%
Moderate	70	21%
Good	236	71%
Grand Total	333	100%

Figure 5.2

Customer Satisfaction of Agent's after-sales service

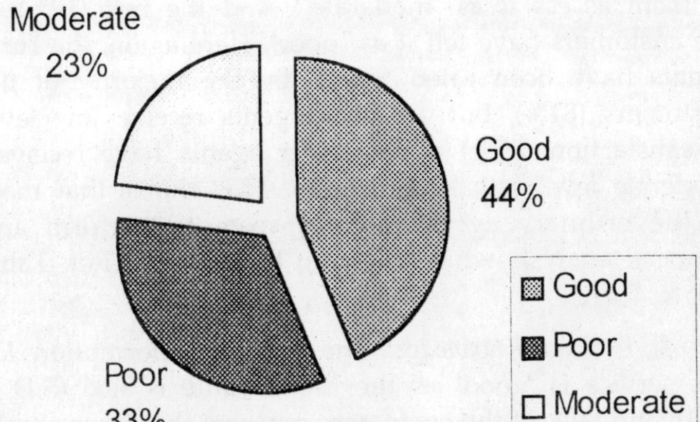

Table 5.2A
Customer Satisfaction and Types of Agents:

Satisfaction	Ordinary Agents		Career Agents		Rural	
	No.	Percentage	No.	Percentage	No.	Percentage
Very Poor	7	4%	1	2%	0	0%
Poor	15	8%	3	6%	2	2%
O.K.	55	28%	11	22%	4	4%
Good	103	52%	27	54%	86	93%
Very Good	18	9%	8	16%	0	0%
Grand Total	198	100%	50	100%	92	100%

2. *Financial Advice:* At the time of selection of policies, the agent is supposed to do counselling on the client's financial needs. To know whether such financial counselling was done while selecting the policy, the customer's perception on this item was obtained which indicates just 'moderate' (Mean=3.42 & S.D=0.84). About 59% customers perceive the service as 'good' and 22% of them assess it as 'moderate'. And the rest (19%) of the customers have felt it as 'poor'. Here again, the rural agents have been rated 'good' by the majority of the customers (81%), but ordinary agents receive low level of satisfaction (47%) while career agents have received moderate level satisfaction (66%). This shows that most of the ordinary agents do not seem to perform any financial analysis while selecting the policies (Ref: Table 5.3 & 5.3A).

3. *Product Knowledge:* The customer perception for this service is 'good' as the Mean value is 3.66 (S.D = 0.84), and 69% of the customers perceive that their agents have a good product knowledge, while 21% of them

Table 5.3
Customer Satisfaction of Financial Advice:

Satisfaction	No	%
Poor	61	19%
Moderate	71	22%
Good	191	59%
Grand Total	323	100%

Table 5.3A
Customer Satisfaction and Types of Agents:

Satisfaction	Ordinary Agents		Career Agents		Rural	
	No.	Percentage	No.	Percentage	No.	%
Very Poor	13	7%	2	4%	0	0%
Poor	30	16%	8	16%	9	10%
O.K.	56	30%	7	14%	8	9%
Good	69	38%	26	52%	74	81%
Very Good	16	9%	7	14%	0	0%
Grand Total	184	100%	50	100%	91	100%

consider it as 'moderate' and the rest (10%) as 'poor'. For rural agents, customer satisfaction is very high (95%) but in case of ordinary agents, it is moderate (54%), while the career agents receive greater satisfaction (79%). This seems to be contradictory to the assumption that rural agents have less product knowledge as compared to urban ordinary agents. Such perception in rural areas might arise possibly because of limited product knowledge (of life insurance) of the customers. And, the career agents having better product knowledge as compared to other agents, confirm the view that the former (career agents) are professionally trained (Ref: Table 5.4 & 5.4A). The inadequate product knowledge of ordinary agents stresses the view that, in the competitive urban financial market which is becoming more sophisticated, the agents

Table 5.4
Customer Satisfaction of Agent's product knowledge:

Satisfaction	No.	%
Poor	33	10%
Moderate	70	21%
Good	230	69%
Grand Total	333	100%

Table 5.4A
Customer Satisfaction and Types of Agents:

Satisfaction	Ordinary Agents		Career Agents		Rural	
	No.	Percentage	No.	Percentage	No.	%
Very Poor	8	4%	0	0%	0	0%
Poor	20	10%	4	8%	2	2%
O.K.	60	31%	7	14%	3	3%
Good	81	42%	31	61%	88	94%
Very Good	24	12%	9	18%	1	1%
Grand Total	193	100%	51	100%	94	100%

should be up-to-date with product knowledge which can help them to compete in the market. Therefore, it has been suggested that more training programmes on various insurance policy plans or schemes as well as other financial products are required to be arranged at regular periodical intervals.

4. *Explaining the details of the policy:* This service has been perceived as 'moderate' (Mean=3.50, & S.D =1.00). The S.D of the data indicates that the perception is

moderately dispersed. Nearly two thirds of customers (64%) are of the view that their agents had explained to them the benefits of policies, in detail, during their initial meetings. Rest of the customers has perceived it either as 'moderate' or 'poor' (18% & 18%). It further shows that maximum number of customers are satisfied with the services of rural agents (89%) and career agents (68%), while the ordinary agents (53%) have been rated as moderate. This suggests that ordinary agents should be given adequate training on various plans by their supervisors (Ref: Table 5.5 & 5.5A).

Table 5.5

Customer Satisfaction over Explanation of product benefits:

Satisfaction	No.	%
Poor	59	18%
Moderate	59	18%
Good	215	65%
Grand Total	333	100%

Table 5.5A

Customer Satisfaction and Types of Agents:

Satisfaction	Ordinary Agents		Career Agents		Rural	
	No.	Percentage	No.	Percentage	No.	%
Very Poor	18	9%	0	0%	0	0%
Poor	27	14%	7	15%	7	8%
O.K.	48	25%	8	17%	3	3%
Good	83	43%	21	45%	83	89%
Very Good	19	10%	11	23%	0	0%
Grand Total	195	100%	47	100%	93	100%

5. *Attentive to the clients:* To know how attentive are the agents to their customer requests, the respondents were asked to comment on this item. The overall perception is mere 'moderate' as it has a low mean value of 3.40, with a moderate dispersion (S.D = 1.04). 61% of customers feel that 'their agents are attentive to their service requirements'. And, nearly 24% of them are of the view that the same is 'poor', while 15% perceive it as 'moderate'. Rural agents have received a high satisfaction (84%), while career agents (56%) and ordinary agents (52%) receive moderate satisfaction (Ref: Table 5.6 & 5.6A).

Table 5.6
Customer Satisfaction of Agent's Attentiveness:

Satisfaction	No.	%
Poor	77	24%
Moderate	48	15%
Good	198	61%
Grand Total	323	100%

Table 5.6A
Customer Satisfaction and Types of Agents:

Satisfaction	Ordinary Agents		Career Agents		Rural	
	No.	Percentage	No.	Percentage	No.	%
Very Poor	17	9.09%	2	4.44%	0	0.00%
Poor	38	20.32%	10	22.22%	10	10.87%
O.K.	35	18.72%	8	17.78%	5	5.43%
Good	79	42.25%	16	35.56%	77	83.70%
Very Good	18	9.63%	9	20.00%	0	0.00%
Grand Total	187	100.00%	45	100.00%	92	100.00%

6. *Friendliness:* Friendliness means 'friendliness of service'. The customers' perception on this count, is almost 'good' (Mean=3.71 & S.D= 0.92), as nearly 74% of the customers perceive it as 'good'. Few have felt it as 'moderate' (15%) & 'poor' (11%). As usual, customer satisfaction for rural agents is `greater' (90%). Similarly, in case of career agents also, the perception is good (77%), but it is moderate for the ordinary agents (64%). This very high level of satisfaction across all groups shows that, at the time of selling the policies, agents have friendly attitude with the customers (Ref: Table 5.7 & 5.7A).

Table 5.7
Customer Satisfaction of Agent's Friendliness:

Satisfaction	No.	%
Poor	38	11%
Moderate	50	15%
Good	244	74%
Grand Total	332	100%

Table 5.7A
Customer Satisfaction and Types of Agents:

Satisfaction	Ordinary Agents		Career Agents		Rural	
	No.	Percentage	No.	Percentage	No.	Per
Very Poor	13	7%	0	0%	0	0%
Poor	21	11%	2	4%	2	2%
O.K.	35	18%	9	19%	7	8%
Good	94	48%	24	50%	84	90%
Very Good	31	16%	13	27%	0	0%
Grand Total	194	100%	48	100%	93	100%

7. *Assistance in filling up the forms:* Perception on this service is also found to be 'good' (Mean = 3.79 & S.D = 0.86). Majority (80%) of the customers has perceived the service as 'good', while the rest perceive it as moderate (9%) and poor (11%). About 94% customers have perceived the rural agent's service as 'good'. Similarly, in case of the career agents and the ordinary agents also, the level of satisfaction is as high as 83% and 71% respectively (Ref: Table 5.8 & 5.8A). Here again, such high level of satisfaction could be due to two

Table 5.8
Customer Satisfaction of Agent's assistance in Forms:

Satisfaction	No	%
Poor	36	11%
Moderate	30	9%
Good	257	80%
Grand Total	323	100%

Table 5.8A
Customer Satisfaction and Types of Agents:

Satisfaction	Ordinary Agents		Career Agents		Rural	
	No.	Percentage	No.	Percentage	No.	Per
Very Poor	7	4%	2	4%	0	0%
Poor	20	11%	3	6%	4	4%
O.K.	26	14%	3	6%	2	2%
Good	101	54%	28	60%	87	94%
Very Good	32	17%	11	23%	0	0%
Grand Total	186	100%	47	100%	93	100%

reasons: This service item might have been rated as of general nature rather than a specific service (pre-sale or post-sale), and they might have better experiences at the time of taking the policy.

Factors determining the satisfaction of pre-sales service

It has been assumed that each aspect of pre-sales service would have separate and distinctive impact on customer's satisfaction, and, if the significant service aspects were identified, it would help the management to take necessary improvement efforts. For this purpose, the same pre-sales service items were selected. To identify the factors determining the satisfaction, the factor analysis was used mainly for two reasons: The variables are part of the construct and there is no dependant variable, and the variables are highly inter-related. The factor loadings of varimax factor matrix are given below.

Table 5.9

Rotated Factor Matrix

	Factor I	Factor II
ADVICE	.73*	.38
ASTDOC	.33	.82*
ASTNOT	.11	.87*
ATTEND	.59*	.64*
COMPET	.80*	.23
EXPBENF	.81*	.29
FORMS	.68*	.29
FRIEND	.70*	.40
OTHAFSAL	.33	.82*
REMIT	.31	.83*
REVIEW	.56*	.51*
SELPOL	.84*	.08
Eigen Values	7.00	1.43
% of variance extracted	58.4	11.9
% of cumulative variance	58.4	70.3

*(Note: Factor loadings with .50 or above have been flagged by *)*

This reveals that, 'of the items significantly loaded in factor I, Selection of policy (.84), Explaining the policy benefits (.81), and Product knowledge (.80) are in the order of high significance closely measuring the latent continuum (pre-sales service). This shows the significance of professionalism on agent's pre-sales service, as they are the basic traits of professionalism. Therefore, if these basic traits of professionalism were improved among agents, it would definitely increase the customer satisfaction over the agent's pre-sales service, which can further result into increased business.

Measurement of agent's after sales services

Agents are supposed to take care of their client's service requirements after selling the policies. Providing satisfactory after-sales service is one of the duties and responsibilities of agents, and for which they receive 'renewal commission'. Even though the operating offices of LIC perform the service, for majority of the customers, the agents serve as their representatives in getting the services done, and they are considered as the initial service providers as far as the customers are concerned. So, it was felt essential to know how the policyholders perceive this service. To measure this perception, the following service items were selected:

(1) Agents' visits to their customers.

(2) Reviewing the insurance needs of their clients.

(3) Assistance in remittance of premium.

(4) Assistance in premium notice.

(5) Assistance in policy documents.

(6) Assistance in other after-sales services.

The policyholders were asked to rate their agents' service in this regard. Since all these items measure the construct, over-all perception score of the after-sales service was obtained by averaging the scores of all the services *(over-all score = policy documents + remittance of premium + premium notice + review of insurance needs + attentive to customers + other after-sales services).*

Customer satisfaction of after-sales service

From Figure 5.2, it is clear that the overall perception is mere 'moderate' (Mean=3.11, and S.D=1.05), as only 44% of the customers have perceived it as 'good'. About 23% and 33% have perceived the service as 'moderate' and 'poor'. The analysis further shows that the service of rural agents has been rated as 'slightly good', while the career agents and ordinary agents are rated as 'moderate' (Ref: Table 5.10 & 5.10A). It was also

Table 5.10

Customer Satisfaction of Agent's after-sales service:

Satisfaction	No	%
Poor	68	33%
Moderate	48	23%
Good	90	44%
Grand Total	206	100%

Table 5.10A

Customer Satisfaction and Types of Agents:

Types of Agent	Mean perception
Ordinary Agents	2.97
Career Agents	3.32
Rural Agents	3.81

observed that, whenever the rural customers visited the branch office for any service, their agents accompanied them. Greater satisfaction for rural agents than for the career-agents indicates that, mere possession of good product knowledge is not sufficient for giving satisfactory service, but the visit to the customers on regular basis is also equally important. Comparing the perception of after-sales service with the pre-sale-service shows that, at the time of selling the policies the agents are showing more interest. But when it comes to after-sales service, they are found to be moderate. It is believed that 'servicing the clients' adds to their profit through additional business'. It also provides them competitive edge over the others. Therefore, it is suggested that the agents should make the use of `relationship marketing' more effectively. And, the supervisory staff (i.e. Development officers and Branch managers) should encourage them to do so by regular nurturing both in field as well as in their training.

Satisfaction of after-sales service items

1. *Agent's Visits:* Most of the agents do not seem to be visiting the customers frequently after their first sale, since nearly 42% of the respondents say that their agents do not turn-up after selling the first policy, and 32% of them feel that only on a very few occasions they visited. About 26% of the respondents are of the opinion that their agents visit them frequently. However, rural agents seem to be visiting the customers frequently as nearly 46% of the respondents have felt it so, and 26% of them said 'their agents occasionally visit them'. However, about 28% of the respondents anguished that their agents never turned up after selling the policies. But in urban areas, it is totally different as only 17% of ordinary agents and 23% of career agents meet their clients frequently. The

percentage of not meeting the customers are high for both career agents (40%) and ordinary agents (50%) (Ref: Table 5.11 & 5.11A). This shows that in urban areas, the agents are interested only in selling the policies. Since the market is becoming very competitive, the agents have to meet their clients more at regular intervals, which can help them in getting not only additional business, but also referrals.

Table 5.11
Customer Satisfaction over Agent's visits:

Duration of visits	No	%
Never	153	42%
Sometimes	115	32%
Frequently	93	26%
Grand Total	361	100%

Table 5.11A
Customer Satisfaction and Types of Agents:

Satisfaction	Ordinary Agents		Career Agents		Rural	
	No.	Percentage	No.	Percentage	No.	%
Frequently	37	17%	12	23%	44	46%
Occasionaly	71	33%	19	37%	25	26%
Never	106	50%	21	40%	26	27%
Grand Total	214	100%	52	100%	95	100%

2. *Reviewing the insurance needs of customers:* Review of the insurance needs of customers refers to how the agents assess their client's insurance needs for additional policies. The mean perception (Mean=2.89 and S.D=1.19) shows that the customers are moderately satisfied on this service. Nearly 42% of them have said that their agents did not do any kind of review on their needs, when 16% of them perceive the service as 'moderate' and the rest 42% as 'good'. The S.D shows that their perception is fairly dispersed, which might be due to the varied quality of service from the agents. In rural areas, as many as 71% of the customers agreed that their agents have enquired them about their additional insurance requirements. Of these, many stated that their agents have also made frequent visits. But in the case of the career agents, nearly 49% of them have expressed that 'their agent's service on this, is 'poor'. The same perception appears in ordinary agents also (48%). Thus, only a small percentage (30%) of the customers are satisfied with this service (Ref: Table 5.12 & 5.12A).

Table 5.12
Customer Satisfaction on Review of insurance needs:

Satisfaction	No	%
Poor	137	42%
Moderate	54	16%
Good	137	42%
Grand Total	328	100%

Table 5.12A
Customer Satisfaction and Types of Agents:

Satisfaction	Ordinary Agents		Career Agents		Rural	
	No.	Percentage	No.	Percentage	No.	%
Very Poor	41	21.69%	9	20.00%	0	0.00%
Poor	50	26.46%	13	28.89%	24	25.53%
O.K.	41	21.69%	10	22.22%	3	3.19%
Good	47	24.87%	8	17.78%	67	71.28%
Very Good	10	5.29%	5	11.11%	0	0.00%
Grand Total	189	100.00%	45	100.00%	94	100.00%

3. *Assistance in remittance of premiums:* In India, even though the agents are not authorised by the LIC to collect premiums, quite a few of them do so as part of their services. The overall perception of the customers on this count has been rated as 'moderate' (Mean=3.37, S.D=1.18). About 61% of them perceive the service as 'good', and 15% of the customers feel it as 'moderate'. Nearly 24% of them have rated the service as 'poor'. Here again, a very high percentage (94%) of the rural customers are pleased with their agents' service, while for career agents & ordinary agents, only a moderate group of customers (62% & 49%) are satisfied. Such greater satisfaction over the rural agents could be because, customers come from a longer distance to the offices for the remittance, and moreover, they mostly know their agents. So, they might expect them to do the needful (Ref: Table 5.13 & 5.13A).

4. *Assistance in premium notice:* It is expected that, when a customer does not get a premium notice from the office, he might seek the help of his agents in getting

Table 5.13
Customer Satisfaction over Remittance of premium:

Satisfaction	No	%
Poor	57	24%
Moderate	36	15%
Good	146	61%
Grand Total	239	100%

Table 5.13A
Customer Satisfaction and Types of Agents:

Satisfaction	Ordinary Agents		Career Agents		Rural	
	No.	Percentage	No.	Percentage	No	%
Very Poor	22	14.67%	5	13.51%	0	0.00%
Poor	22	14.67%	5	13.51%	3	5.77%
O.K.	32	21.33%	4	10.81%	0	0.00%
Good	54	36.00%	17	45.95%	49	94.23%
Very Good	20	13.33%	6	16.22%	0	0.00%
Grand Total	150	100.00%	37	100.00%	52	100.00%

the same. Knowledge about how the agents are assisting the customers in this regard would be very helpful for improving the service. Customer's perception on the service is found to be 'moderate' (Mean=3.10, and S.D=1.24). Nearly 47% of them perceive the service as 'good' and 19% of the customers feel it as 'moderate'. About 34% of them have perceived it as 'poor'. In case of rural agents, very high level of satisfaction (94%) exists, whereas in career agents (52%) and ordinary agents (40%), it is moderate (Ref: Table 5.14 & 5.14A). This indicates that in urban areas, even such simple service is not being provided satisfactorily, when they are supposed to ensure their clients' policies in-force.

5. *Assistance in policy documents:* This refers to the extent of agent's assistance in obtaining the policy

Table 5.14
Customer Satisfaction of Agent's assistance in Premium notice:

Satisfaction	No	%
Poor	59	34%
Moderate	33	19%
Good	83	47%
Grand Total	175	100%

Table 5.14A
Customer Satisfaction and Types of Agents:

Satisfaction	Ordinary Agents		Career Agents		Rural	
	No.	Percentage	No.	Percentage	No.	%
Very Poor	19	14.62%	6	22.22%	0	0.00%
Poor	32	24.62%	1	3.70%	1	5.56%
O.K.	27	20.77%	6	22.22%	0	0.00%
Good	40	30.77%	8	29.63%	17	94.44%
Very Good	12	9.23%	6	22.22%	0	0.00%
Grand Total	130	100.00%	27	100.00%	18	100.00%

documents for their customers. The mean perception of this service is 'moderate' (Mean=3.26, S.D=1.17), as 51% of the customers are satisfied, and 26% are dissatisfied. On this service also, the customer satisfaction has been 'moderate' for both the career agents and the ordinary agents (67% and 45%) as compared to rural agents where it is as high as 92% (Ref: Table 5.15 & 5.15A).

6. *Other After-Sales Services.* Under this, all the other after-sales services such as assistance in getting maturity claims, loans, nominations and assignments, survival

Table 5.15

Customer Satisfaction over Assistance in Policy Documents:

Satisfaction	No	%
Poor	51	26%
Moderate	47	24%
Good	102	51%
Grand Total	200	100%

Table 5.15A

Customer Satisfaction and Types of Agents:

Satisfaction	Ordinary Agents		Career Agents		Rural	
	No.	Percentage	No.	Percentage	No.	%
Very Poor	21	13.38%	1	3.33%	0	0.00%
Poor	23	14.65%	5	16.67%	1	7.69%
O.K.	43	27.39%	4	13.33%	0	0.00%
Good	53	33.76%	15	50.00%	12	92.31%
Very Good	17	10.83%	5	16.67%	0	0.00%
Grand Total	157	100.00%	30	100.00%	13	100.00%

benefit payments, revivals, surrenders, etc. were included. The customers' over-all perception on this found to be 'moderate' as the mean value (Mean=2.93, S.D=1.26) is in the moderate range. Nearly 42% of them perceive the service as 'good', and 18% of the respondents feel it as 'moderate'. About 40% of them perceive it as 'poor'. In this service also, the rural agents seem to be the satisfactory providers (83%). The services of the career agents and the ordinary agents are rated as 'moderate' (53% & 40%) (Ref: Table 5.16 & 5.16A).

Table 5.16
Customer Satisfaction of Agent's other services:

Satisfaction	No	%
Poor	71	41%
Moderate	31	18%
Good	73	42%
Grand Total	175	100%

Table 5.16A
Customer Satisfaction of other after sales services:

Satisfaction	Ordinary Agents		Career Agents		Rural	
	No.	Percentage	No.	Percentage	No.	%
Poor	65	34%	10	21%	5	5%
Moderate	50	26%	12	26%	11	12%
Good	78	40%	25	53%	78	83%
Grand Total	193	100%	47	100%	94	100%

Factors determining the satisfaction of after-sales service

It has been felt essential to identify the significant factors determining the satisfaction of after-sale service that can help in prioritising the improvement efforts. Since these service items are the basic determinants of after-sales service, and are inter-related to each other, the factor analysis (Ref: Table 5.9) was used for this purpose. The factor loadings of the varimax rotated factor matrix have revealed the following findings:

'Timely sending of premium notices' is the most significant factor in determining the satisfaction of after-sales service. This shows that the policyholders regard this as the most important service that they expect their

agents to ensure that these notices are sent regularly. But the agents' service on this, has been 'mere moderate', the agents are advised to ensure total satisfaction which can minimise the chances of lapsation of policies. The next significant factor is *'timely assistance in remitting the premiums for the customers'*. On this count also, the agents' service is 'moderate'. And, *'Assistance in getting intermediary or ancillary services'* such as getting the policy documents, loan, and interim payments (money back policy) etc., has been found as the third important factor.

Summary

The assessment of agent's service indicated that customer satisfaction of both pre-sales as well as the after-sales services was 'moderate', In particular, the low-moderate satisfaction of after-sales service as compared to the pre-sales service is the immediate concern for improvement. The analysis further revealed that 'professionalism' is the important factor in determining the satisfaction. In case of the after-sales services, timely sending of premium notices, timely assistance in premium remittances, and providing satisfactory intermediary services, were found as the important determinants of satisfaction. The next chapter deals with assessment of office service and identification of factors determining the satisfaction of office service.

Chapter 6

OFFICE SERVICE SATISFACTION AND MEASUREMENT

Introduction

The service quality perceptions, to a greater extent, depend on the experience of various service dimensions during the service process. Customer satisfaction of service is determined by the overall judgement of their experiences on various service encounters. While experiencing these service encounters the number of elements or dimensions such as: tangibility, reliability, responsiveness, empathy, etc. would have a greater impact on their satisfactions. Parasuraman, Zeithaml, and Berry (1985)[1] identified 10 determinants of the service quality: reliability, responsiveness, competence, access, courtesy, communication, credibility, security, understanding the customer and tangibles. Their study on 'service quality' has revealed that these service dimensions have a significant impact on the perceived service quality of customers. Evert Gummessan[2] says 'Quality is not just the output of a rational, logical, and impersonal productive system. As service evolves in interaction with customers; empathy, a caring personality, desire to serve, emotions, involvement, compassion, sense of humour, facet of knowledge and intuition - all dimensions of the love factor - become essential, even the decisive contributors to service quality'. The International Standard ISO 9000(1990)[3] defines the quality as "totality of features and characteristics of a product or service that bear on its ability to satisfy stated and implied needs".

All these views indicate that quality result, not from a particular feature of service, it relies on totality of all features. Therefore, in this study, customer satisfaction of the services of operating offices of LIC has been measured through an instrument (SERVPERF) incorporating all important service dimensions from the customers' perceptions/point of view.

Measurement of Office services

Initially, Delphi method was used to identify the various service items for the measurement. In this regard, several discussions were held with the policyholders, contact-service people (ClassIII employees), departmental heads, marketing officials, and managers of LIC. The service items identified for the measurement are listed below:

1. Appearance of the branch,
2. Convenient operating hours,
3. Directing the customers to a proper person,
4. Adequacy of job knowledge,
5. Explaining the procedures clearly,
6. Informing the time duration for completion of work,
7. Time taken for completion of work,
8. Replying the customer's letters immediately,
9. Attending to the work immediately,

10. When the concerned employee is not available, others attend the work,
11. Unnecessary visits for completion of work,
12. Keeping up the service promises,
13. Error-free and accurate service,
14. Courtesy and politeness,
15. Customer friendliness,
16. Helping the customers in filling up the forms,
17. Showing adequate interest in the customer's work,
18. Understanding the customer's service needs in the circumstantial context,
19. Simple systems and procedures,
20. Maintenance of customer records,
21. Involving more number of people for single service causes delay*
22. Sincerity of the employees towards the assigned work*

For measuring these service items, an instrument called 'SERVPERF'** was developed. In developing the instrument, the well-established procedures designed by A. Parasuraman and others were followed. Ten service quality dimensions were developed using the above 22 service items. Then, agreement statements relevant for these items were constructed, and six-point scale ranging from 1(strongly agree) to 6 (strongly disagree) was accompanied to each statement. This instrument was tested for validation by carrying-out pilots study with the sample size of 60 policyholders, at a LIC branch office in Pune. This pilot study helped in dropping the items that were found to be overlapping and difficult to measure, and some items were modified. Finally, the following 20 items were retained in the final instrument for this study, which have been categorised into 10 dimensions;

1. *Tangibility:* Appearance of the branch.

2. *Accessibility:* Convenient operating hours, Directing the customers to a proper person.
3. *Competence:* Adequacy of job knowledge.
4. *Communication:* Explaining the procedures clearly.
5. *Assurance:* Informing the time duration for completion of work.
6. *Responsiveness:* Time taken for completion of work, Attending to the work immediately, Replying the customer letters immediately, When the concerned employee is not available, others attend the work, Unnecessary visits for completion of work,
7. *Reliability:* Keeping up the service promises, Error-free and accurate service.
8. *Empathy:* Courtesy and politeness, Customer friendliness, Helping the customers in filling-up the forms, Showing interest in customer's work.
9. *System and procedures:* Simple systems and procedures, Maintenance of customer records.
10. *Understanding the customer:* Understanding the customer's service needs in thecircumstantial context.

The mean satisfaction ratings for these dimensions were obtained by averaging the scores of the items forming the respective dimensions. The SERVPERF score, which is an over-all score for office service, was obtained by averaging the mean scores of all dimensions.

Reliability of the SERVPERF

To know the reliability of the scale Cronbach's alpha reliability test was performed by using SPSS software

Table 6.1
Reliability Analysis - Scale (ALPHA)
Item-total Statistics

	Scale mean if them delected	Scale variance if them delected	Corrected item total correlation	alphsa if them delected
Appear	77.6451	256.9492	.3891	.9177
HRS	77.6512	256.0243	.3548	.9188
Direct	77.7864	249.3034	.4612	.9168
Know	77.5648	258.4740	0.833	.9176
Proc	77.5553	248.5608	.6118	.9133
Assur	78.3188	244.7250	.5422	.9149
Time	78.1686	242.5367	.5955	.9135
Reply	78.3369	248.0920	.5090	.9155
Attend	77.8064	241.4447	.7243	.9106
Othattnd	78.1540	243.6384	.6092	.9131
Vismore	78.0618	238.8240	.6478	.9122
Promise	77.9809	246.9371	.5543	.9144
Accur	77.8836	243.4216	.6649	.9119
Court	77.5777	247.2715	.6516	.9125
Friend	77.5790	248.4822	.6148	.9132
Help	77.7312	243.7437	.7189	.9110
Inrst	77.7630	241.6703	.7756	.9097
Undstand	77.9296	246.3577	.5808	.9138
System	77.8513	250.1544	.4975	.9157
Record	77.8422	242.3553	.6273	.9127

Reliability Coefficients
N of Cases = 232.0 N of Items = 20
Alpha = .9179

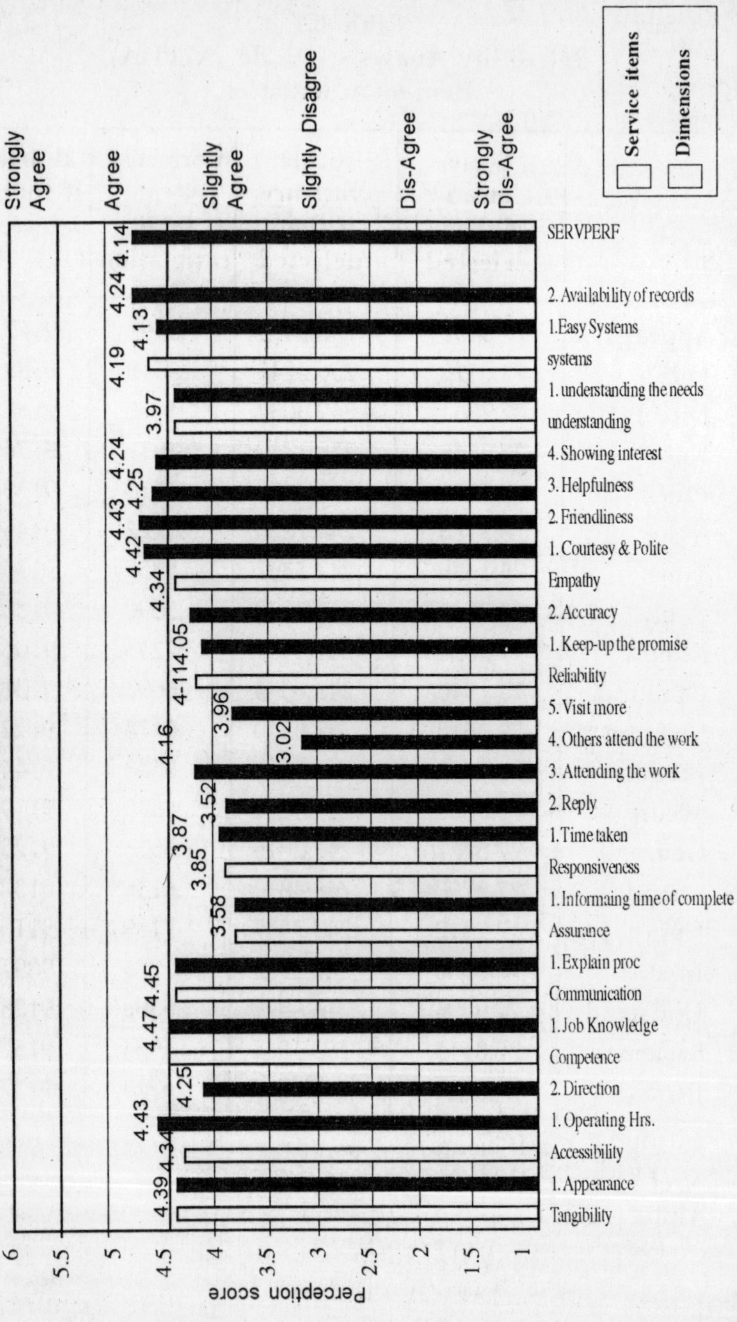

Chart 6.1 Office Service Satisfaction

package. The alpha reliability value for the scale is 0.92 (Being a Coefficient, the maximum value of alpha does not exceed 1). This shows high reliability for the scale since it exceeds the Cronbach's criteria of 0.70. (Ref. Table 6.1)

Customer satisfaction of the Office service

The overall satisfaction of the customers show a 'moderate satisfaction' with the services of the operating offices of LIC, as the mean satisfaction rating is just 4.14 on six point scale. The Standard Deviation (0.27) of the data shows that most of the customers are of the same perception. Moreover, the customer satisfaction is moderate for almost all the service dimensions.

The customer satisfaction of the service dimensions shows that Assurance and Responsiveness are in lower level of moderate satisfaction. The mean satisfaction score for Assurance is 3.68 on a six-point scale. This indicates that on most occasions, the service people are not able to give any kind of assurance to their customers about when the services would be completed. The next service dimension which has the second lowest score is Responsiveness (Mean=3.86). Of the responsive items, Employee's reply to the customer letters (3.52), attentiveness of other employee's when the concerned employee is not available (4.16), the time taken for completion of work (3.87) were rated as low-moderate, while attending the clients (4.16), and delivering the service at fewer visits (3.96) are perceived to be just moderate.

The service dimensions: Reliability (4.11), System (4.19), Accessibility (4.34) Empathy (4.34), and Understanding the customers (3.97) have been perceived as moderately satisfied. Of the service items, Keeping-up of the service promises (4.05) and Understanding the customers (3.97) have received comparatively low ratings.

However, Tangibility (4.39), Communication (4.45), and Employee's competency (4.47) have been perceived as comparatively better (Ref: Chart 6.1). This shows that the office performance needs to be improved on all the service dimensions, but improving Assurance, Responsiveness, Reliability, Understanding the customer's service needs in the circumstantial context, and System, is of immediate concern, since the market itself is becoming quality driven and very competitive.

Factors determining the satisfaction of office service

Though the literature and empirical studies on service quality support, using the aforesaid ten dimensions for assessing the service performance of an office, it would be quite useful to the management if statistically significant factors are identified, so that they can prioritise their improvement efforts. To identify significant factors, the Factor Analysis was selected as an appropriate method since the ten dimensions are inter-related. To know the inter-relations of the dimensions, a correlation matrix of the same was obtained which reveals that:

i) There is a high degree of correlation among Responsiveness, Assurance and Reliability items,

ii) All the empathy items are highly correlated,

iii) System, help, accuracy and records are also correlated.

These results suggest for using Factor Analysis to identify the factors accounting for the interrelationships among the variables.

Accordingly, the Factor Analysis using PCA with urban and rural data was done separately. In case of urban, the PCA has extracted four factors explaining 59% cumulative variation. The first factor explains 41% variation, second and third factors explain 7% and 6% respectively. And, the fourth factor explains 5% variation. Since the factor matrix obtained through PCA does not give a simple and clear structure, the factors were rotated for varimax rotation. The rotated factor matrix gives an interesting and meaningful structure that is Table in 6.2:

On the basis of the meaning of the variables significantly loaded, the factors were named as FactorI -Empathy, FactorII -Responsiveness, FactorIII - System, and FactorIV Tangibility.

Factor I: Empathy: This factor explains 41% variation, so it can be considered as the most significant factor for customer satisfaction. In this factor: courtesy and politeness, friendliness, individual attention, helping the customers in filling-up the forms, explaining the procedures clearly, and understanding the customer's service needs in circumstantial context have been significantly loaded. This conveys that these items are perceived as very important while evaluating the office service. Therefore, LIC should periodically monitor the office performance on this factor (empathy) and wherever necessary, improvement efforts should be taken up.

Factor II: Responsiveness: This factor explains the time factor or responsiveness of employees (quickness of services). In this factor, the following items have been very significantly loaded: timely completion of service, replying the customer letters immediately, completion of work at fewer visits, attending to the work immediately, and informing the time duration for completion of work. This indicates that timeliness of service (responsiveness)

Table 6.2

Rotated Factor matrix:

	FactorI	FactorII	FactorIII	FactorIV
APPEAR	28	14	-05	74*
HRS	10	-03	59	60*
DIRECT	27	48	13	-01
KNOW	54*	01	19	-08
PROC	65*	23	07	24
ASSUR	06	63*	14	51
TIME	28	74*	06	02
REPLY	03	73*	12	30
ATTEND	62	43*	18	13
OTHATTND	47	32	36	12
VISMORE	30	65*	29	04
PROMISE	48	46	07	-04
ACCUR	49	35	51*	-03
COURT	77*	17	06	22
FRIEND	73*	11	21	11
HELP	68*	27	25	23
INRST	69*	37	26	16
UNDSTAND	57*	44	-10	10
SYSTEM	20	21	77*	05
RECORD	42	45	42*	-11
Eigen Values.	8.11	1.35	1.16	1.05
% of variance extracted.	41	7	6	5
Cumulative % of variance.	41	48	54	59

Note:

1. *The printed values are multiplied by 100 and rounded to the nearest integer. Values greater than 50have been flagged by an *,*
2. *Items having a factor loading of 50 or above are considered as significantly loaded in a particular factor, and where an item is loaded in more than one factor significantly, that item has been taken into a factor where it has a greatest loading,*
3. *Items having negative signs (-) are not taken,*
4. *Since these items* have a loading of above 40 and related to the factors on empirical and conceptual grounds, they were grouped into the respective factors.*

seems to be the secondary factor for the urban policyholders as it explains only 7% variation.

Factor III: System This factor represents service systems and procedures of an office. The service items prominently loaded are simple systems and procedures of service, error free and accurate service, and maintenance of policy records. This stresses the importance of simple systems and procedures in providing satisfactory service. The impact of this factor on satisfaction is 6%.

Factor IV: Tangibles: This factor explains tangibles of service that account for only 5% variation. Appearance of office and convenient operating hours are significantly loaded in this factor. Since only two items are significantly loaded in this factor, it has been considered as insignificant according to Kaiser's criteria. This shows that this factor has a very low impact on customer satisfaction.

Factors influencing the satisfaction of rural customers

To identify the significant service dimensions in case of rural policyholders, the factor analysis using PCA was done. The PCA has extracted 6 factors explaining a cumulative percentage of 70% variation. Examination of these factors has revealed that the factor pattern is not meaningful and clear, the factor loadings were rotated for promax rotation. The rotated factor structure is given below for interpretation;

Examination of these factor loadings shows that three factors are significant according to Kaiser's criteria and the same together explains 50% variation, which also reveals its significance. Factor-I represents Responsiveness, Factor-II represents Organisational Competency and Factor-III explains Empathy.

Table 6.3

Rotation method: Promax

Factor Structure:

	FACTOR1	FACTOR2	FACTOR3*	FACTOR4*	FACTOR5*	FACTOR6*
TIME	80 *	16	32	13	-6	16
HELP	79 *	32	11	12	-8	-24
VISMORE	78 *	45	16	25	-9	4
ATTEND	76 *	53	37	26	-17	-7
OTHAVAIL	47 *	-3	2	1	2	39
HRS	39	81 *	-9	27	-17	-32
ACCUR	37	83 *	41	19	-12	8
KNOW	22	72 *	57	4	-1	-1
ASSUR	11	60 *	29	37	-24	1
RECOR	35	33	83 *	-12	-10	13
REPLY	5	19	72 *	22	-20	-2
INRST	65	38	74 *	15	-1	-10
COURT	40	64	64 *	36	-9	5
DIRECT	14	20	13	91 *	-17	-24
PROC	30	36	1	77 *	-6	32
APPEAR	1	1	1	-1	88*	6
PROMISE	58 *	51	28	27	-61	1
FRIEND	23	42	52 *	40	-74	-2
UNDSTAND	26	30	21	12	4	61*
SYSTEM	39	40 *	17	19	-1	-67
Eigen values	6.12	2.00	1.77	1.48	1.35	1.15
% of variance extracted.	31	10	9	7	7	6
Cumulative % of variance.	31	41	50	57	64	70

Note:

1. *Printed values are multiplied by 100 and rounded to the nearest integer. Values greater than 50 have been flagged by an* *
2. *Items having a factor loading of 50 or above are considered as significantly loaded in a particular factor. Where an item is loaded in more than one factor significantly, that item has been taken into a factor in which it has the greatest loading.*
3. *Factors with* indicate that they failed to qualify as significant factors according to Kaiser's criteria: A factor should have a minimum of 3 items with significant loading.*
4. *Items having negative signs (-) are not taken.*
5. *Since these items(have a loading of above 40 and related to the factors on empirical and conceptual grounds, they were grouped into the respective factors.*

Of these, *Factor-I Responsiveness* can be considered as the most significant factor as it explains maximum variation (31%). In this, timely service, completion of service at fewer visits, attending to the customers immediately, and when the concerned employee is not available-other's attentiveness, and performing the service at the promised time are significantly loaded. This shows that rural customers consider 'Employee's responsiveness in giving timely service as the most important factor while evaluating the office service. This could be because in rural areas the customers come from the distant places to the branch, so when they want to get any service, they expect it to be delivered quickly. As this factor alone contributes 31% to satisfaction, improving this factor would enhance the customer satisfaction to a greater extent.

Factor-II represents Organisational Competency. This factor explains 10% variation. In this, Error-free and accurate service, Convenient operating hours, Adequacy of service knowledge and skills, Assurance, and System and procedures are significantly loaded. This reveals that the rural customers expect the operating offices to possess these competencies as a pre-requisite for satisfactory service.

Factor-III represents Empathy (Customer concern): The 9% variation explained by this factor shows that it has low level impact on satisfaction (whereas the same factor has been found very significant among the urban customers). However, the significance of this factor suggests that providing timely service with empathy can make the customers more delightful.

Summary

This analysis revealed that in an over-all consideration and analysis, the two service dimensions that are commonly deficient and perceived 'unsatisfactory' by the customers are Assurance, and Responsiveness. The other service dimensions that were perceived high in importance by the customers, are Reliability, Communication, Access, and System. Moderate satisfactions were found on Empathy and Understanding the customer needs. The factor analysis revealed that in urban areas, 'Empathy' has been emerged as very important factor in determining the satisfaction of office service, while Responsiveness, System, and Tangibles were, though important, found secondary. However, in rural area, Responsiveness has been found as a significant factor, and organisational competency and Empathy were found as secondary determinants. In the next chapter, a service quality model has been developed to study the linear relationships of the service quality parameters. An index has also been created to measure the service quality in totality for the operating offices of LIC

REFERENCES

* Items with* indicate that they were dropped after pilot study.

** The SERVPERF scale has been given under Q12 of the Questionnaire.

1. Parasuraman A., Valarie A. Zeithaml, and Leonard Berry (1985), "A Conceptual Model of Service Quality and its Implications for Further Research," Journal of Marketing, 48 (Fall), P. 41-50.

2. Gummesson E. (1991), "Service Quality - A Holistic View," in Service Quality: Multidisciplinary and Multinational Perspectives, Brown S.W., Gummesson E., Edvardsson E., and Gustavsson B. (eds.), Lexington, MA: Lexington Books, P. 3.

3. Dennis Green (1996), The complete ISO 9000 Manual, London: Kogan Page Ltd., P. 13.

Chapter 7

DEVELOPMENT OF SERVICE QUALITY INDEX

Introduction

This chapter analysis the relationship of the service quality parameters: Product satisfaction, Agent's satisfaction, Agent's service, Office service and Overall service, with a view to develop a service quality model. It is also attempted to create an index to measure the total service quality in life insurance.

Setting of Hypotheses for Development of the Model

Life insurance is generally perceived as an abstract in nature and latent in need. Customer's knowledge about life insurance products is also very less. Even now, with the advent of information explosion and market developments, most of the customers experience difficulties in understanding the life insurance terminology, determining the policy type, coverage, etc. Hence, the customers expect their agents be more knowledgeable and competent enough to provide certain pre-sales services such as explaining the benefits of various policies, selection of appropriate policy, counseling of financial needs, etc., at the time of taking a policy. Because these pre-sales services are considered as important and are performed at the initial stage in converting the prospective customers into the customers of LIC, how well these services are performed by the agents may have an impact on customer's perception of service quality. If one gets dissatisfaction at this point, the 'hello effect' may continue to affect his perception of the subsequent services.

To what extent, this will affect the customer's perception needs some examination because, perceiving this service as important, is subjective and personal, which may vary from individual to individual. It is believed that this will have a greater impact only on product satisfaction, not on other services. Therefore, it is felt necessary to study the hypothesis (H1) that *"Agent's pre-sales service would have an impact on customer perception of subsequent services"*.

Life Insurance is bought for various needs viz. risk benefit, tax benefit, savings for the future, for getting loan, etc. So, during the policy period, if the product fails to fulfil the need for which it was bought, it may cause some dissatisfaction to the customers. Generally speaking, Life insurance should not be compared with other financial products, since the former being entirely a different product with the basic benefit of risk cover. But, most of the people purchase life insurance mainly for future savings rather than for risk protection. So, in their opinion, it is a financial product with an expectation of better return, safety and liquidity. Moreover, market sophistication and intensive competition in the financial market have made the life insurance policyholders to expect high return from LIC also. Under these circumstances, customer's general perception about life insurance (risk product / financial product) would have a significant impact on product satisfaction. Sometimes, life insurance policy is bought under agent's compulsion, though the customer has no need for the product. In some cases, the agents, in order to get more commission or complete the business quota, insist the customers to insure for an amount more than their financial capacity - which is known as 'over selling'. Such cases may create product dissatisfaction among the policyholders. These, to what extent, affect the perceptions of subsequent services need to be examined as it can aid for the necessary improvement of the same. These issues make it necessary to study the hypothesis (H2) that *"Product satisfaction would have a perceptible impact on customer perception of subsequent services"*.

After buying the life insurance policy, the policyholders are required to avail of certain after-sales services during their policy period i.e. issue of policy documents, premium notices and receipts, loan, transfer of policy, claims, etc. When the policyholders need these services, they approach their agents to help them, as they are seen as representatives of LIC. The agents do act as facilitators between the operating offices and the customers in getting these services done. It is one of the responsibilities of the agent as stated in the Agent Regulation Act 1972;'Every agent shall, with a view to conserving the business already secured, maintain contact with all persons who have become policyholders of LIC through him and shall assist them in after-sales services. For which, they get renewal commission'. Since the agents are seen as the representatives of LIC, failure to provide these services to their clients may, not only create dissatisfaction to them, but also affect their perceptions of other services, particularly office services and overall service quality. To what extent, it affects them is a hypothetical one. Because, perceiving the agent as a distinct person or part of LIC is a subjective and personal view. So, those who perceive agent's service as separate and individual may not necessarily relate it while evaluating the organizational service quality. This stresses a need for developing the hypothesis (H3) that *"Agent's after-sales service would have an impact on customer perception of office services and over-all service quality"*.

The Branch Offices of LIC are the centers for sales and policy servicing. The complete services are being rendered at these operating offices. Beside this, they are functioning as a single window sales and service center and have a policyholder's grievance cell. These branches are having adequate financial as well as non-financial powers to render the services with computerized operations. Therefore, when measuring the service quality, it is essential to measure the branch performance on how well the after-sales services are being rendered. Since life insurance is an intangible product, and for a longer term, during the term of the policy what a policyholder gets is only a surety that a lump sum (Sum Assured) will be paid to him/his heir or assignee on maturity/death. So, if these services are not rendered to his satisfaction, it will not only erode his 'faith in the organization, but will also create a doubt in his mind about the final payment which ultimately can affect the Corporation's image.

Some studies on service quality also revealed that measurement of the same includes 'the assessment of customers' experience with the organization and their level of satisfaction with those experiences'. During the process of service delivery, what experience the customer gets is also an important determinant. These experiences include the following service dimensions: tangible aspects of the office, employee's job knowledge, how clearly the service people explain the procedures, time taken to perform the work, responsiveness to customers requirements, reliability in keeping the service promises, having empathy; caring, helpful, individual attention, courtesy, understanding the customer needs, etc. These are the various dimensions of service produced at the office. So, when one experiences the service in the office, how these various dimensions of services are performed by the service people will definitely affect the customer's perceptions of other services i.e. product satisfaction, agent's services, overall service quality, etc. Therefore, it has been felt necessary to study the hypothesis (H4) that *"Office services would have a significant impact on over-all service quality and others"*

Since the main objective of this analysis is to study the linear relationships among the key parameters of service quality, these hypotheses were tested through a model wherein a series of linear equations were studied simultaneously. The specification of the model is given below:

Specification of the Service Quality Model

The model given below explains the causal relationships of the variables in the model. Each path arrow indicates the casual relationship of one variable with the other, is denoted by β's.

It has been hypothesized in the model that Pre-sales service would affect product satisfaction, after-sales service, and office service. Product satisfaction is assumed to affect pre-sale service, after sales service, office service and over-all service quality. Similarly, After sales service has been predicted to influence office service, product satisfaction and over-all service quality. Office service is expected to affect the product satisfaction, after-sales service and over-all service quality.

Figure 7.1 - Service Quality Model

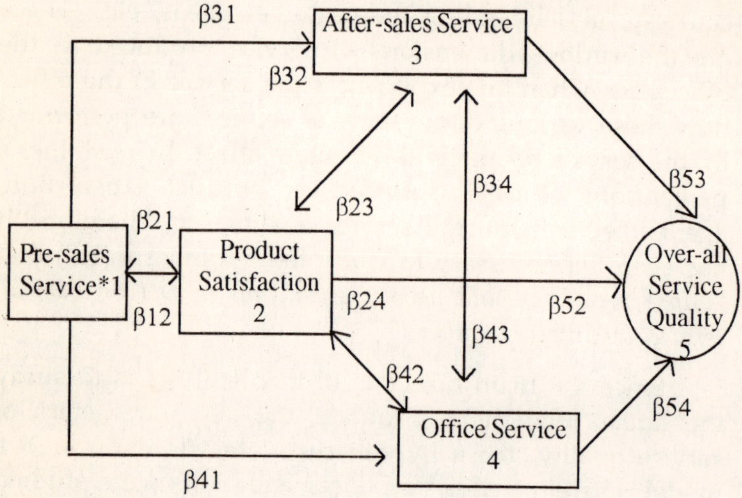

Validating the Model

The above model was validated using a series of regression equations. Relationships of each of these paths were tested by a separate regression where each causing variable was taken as independent variable and the resultant variable had been taken as dependent variable in the equation. The regression equation proved significant relationships for most of the specified paths (Ref: Table 7.1). The analysis revealed the following findings:

Figure 7.2

Modified Service Quality Model

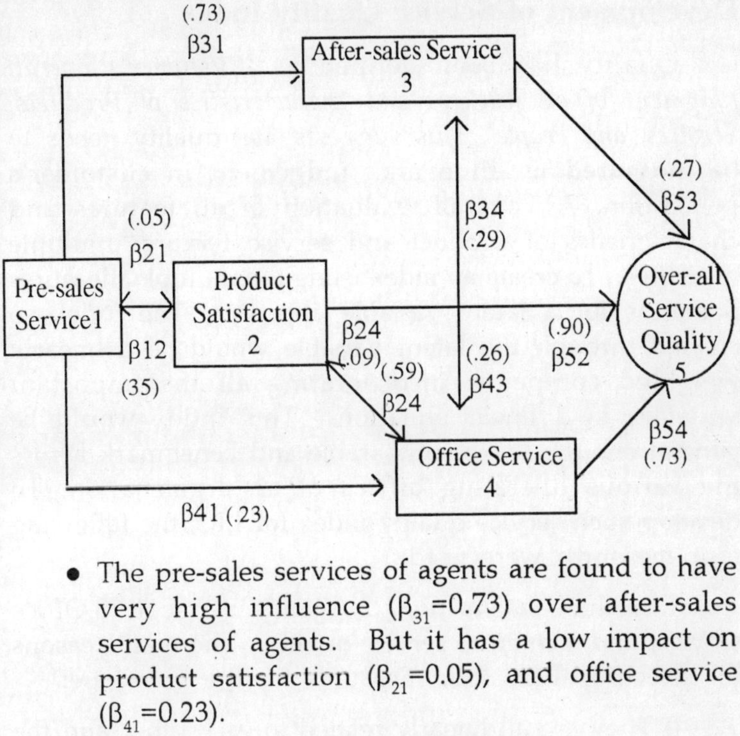

- The pre-sales services of agents are found to have very high influence (β_{31}=0.73) over after-sales services of agents. But it has a low impact on product satisfaction (β_{21}=0.05), and office service (β_{41}=0.23).
- Product satisfaction is found to have greater influence on office service (β_{42}=0.59) and over-all service quality (β_{52}=0.90). It has a moderate impact on pre-sales service (β_{12}=0.35). The paths (β_{32} and β_{23}) between product satisfaction and agent's after-sales services were not significant.
- Agent's after-sales service has low impact over office service (β_{43}=0.26) and over-all quality (β_{53}=0.27).
- Office service is found to have greater influence on over-all quality (β_{54}=0.73), but has lower

impact on both product satisfactions (β_{24}=0.09) and agent's after-sales service (β_{34}=0.29).

Development of Service Quality Index

Quality has been defined as *'Customer's overall judgment of all features and characteristics of Products, Services, and People'*. This suggests that quality needs to be measured as an overall judgement in customer's perception. An overall evaluation of all features and characteristics of product and service requires multiple measures. To create an index using the multiple measures demands for a latent variable approach. The index so created through the latent variable would be a linearly weighted composite incorporating all the important variables in a linear equation. This Index would be general enough to be comparable and benchmark across the various operating offices of an organisation. To develop such service quality index for LIC, the following four measures were used:

1.Product satisfaction, 2.Agent's service1, 3.Office service, and 4.Over-all service quality. The main reasons for selecting these four measures for the index are:

i) They are all linearly related to each other and the index needs to capture that linear relationship,

ii) It has been assumed in life insurance that customer's perceived service quality would depend on product, agent's service and office service, and

iii) The variable 'over-all service quality' has been considered as a separate construct in Marketing literature as it is found to have a separate and distinctive impact, and it is believed to be reflecting more the overall organizational service capabilities than the specific service experiences.

In order to get a linearly weighted composite index, these four measures were factor analyzed by using proc-factor scoring procedure in SAS software (since these measures have different measurement scales, they were standardized before factor analyzing). The proc-factor scoring procedure uses the regression method to create the factor score. The factor score so created is a linear combination of raw data and scoring coefficients (Factor coefficients). For each observation in the raw data set, the factor scoring procedure multiplies the value of a variable in the raw data set by the matching scoring coefficient from the data set of scoring coefficients. This multiplication process is repeated for each variable in the VAR statement. The resulting products are then summed up to produce the value of a new variable. This entire process is repeated for each observation in the raw data set. Thus, an overall composite weighted index was created (Ref: Table 7.1).

Reliability and Validity of the Index

Reliability of the index was tested by using Cronbuch Alpha test. The Alpha Reliability test produced Alpha co-efficient of 0.71, which indicates an acceptable reliability[2]. The validity of the index also was examined by using Factor Analysis. The Factor Analysis confirmed Construct validity, as the average variance extracted by a single factor was 50%[3]. Secondly, the factor loadings to the variables were also high (above 0.50) indicating that the correlation between the indicators and the construct that are supposed to measure, is high. Further validity was also found in the signs and magnitude of the estimated co-efficients. All variable loadings have the expected positive sign and are of high magnitude (Above 0.50) (Ref: Tables 7.1 & 7.2).

Table 7.1

Factor Analysis For Service Quality Index

Initial Factor Method : Principal Components = Prior Communality Estimates: ONE

Eigenvalues of the Correlation Matrix : Total=4Average=1

	1	2	3	4
Eigenvalue	1.997955	0.869841	0.782956	0.349248
Difference	1.128114	0.086884	0.43708	
Proportion	0.50	0.22	0.20	0.08
Cumulative	0.50	0.72	0.92	1.0000

1 factors will be retained by the MINEIGEN criterion.

Factor Pattern

Factor1 (Variance explained by FACTOR1 50%)	
Prosat	0.53581
Agtserv	0.54153
Servperf	0.83026
Servqual	0.85340

Data set from PROC Factor

OBS	Type	Name	Prosat	Agtserv	Servperf	Servqual
1	Mean		1.708	3.468	4.248	3.515
2	STD		0.279	0.749	0.709	0.800
3	N		382.000	382.000	382.000	382.000
4	Communality		0.287	0.293	0.689	0.728
5	Eigenvalue		1.998	0.870	0.783	0.349
6	Prir.c Components (Factor1)		0.536	0.542	0.830	0.853
7	Pattern	Factor1	0.536	0.542	0.830	0.853
8	Score	Factor1	0.268	0.271	0.416	0.427

(Standardized scoring coefficients)

Data set from PROC SCORE

OBS	Prosat	Agtserv	Servperf	Servqual	Factor1
1	1.67	3.47	4.25	4	0.22470
2	2.00	3.47	3.90	3	-0.19720
3	1.67	3.47	5.20	4	0.78184
4	1.67	3.47	4.60	3	-0.10414
5	1.33	3.47	3.60	4	-0.48357

Table 7.2

Reliability Analysis - Scale (ALPHA)

Variables selected for Index :

1. Product Satisfaction,
2. Agent's Pre-sales service,
3. Agent's After-sales service,
4. Office Service,
5. Over all Service Quality.

Item-total Statistics:

Variables	ScaleMean if Item Deleted	Scale variance if Item Deleted	Corrected Item Total Correlation	Alpha If Item Deleted.
Product Satisfaction	14.43	4.76	.31	.69
Pre-sales serivice	12.62	3.37	.49	.63
After-sales service	12.98	3.24	.50	.62
Office service	11.89	3.31	.52	.61
Over all service quality	12.62	3.08	.51	.62

Reliability Coefficients

No of Cases = 382.

Number of Variables = 5

Alpha = 0.71.

Total Service Quality in LIC

The above index was used to measure the Total Service Quality in LIC. The index indicated 'a moderate quality' as the factor scores of majority policyholders (49%) were in moderate range. About 35% policyholders have the scores in 'satisfactory level' and 16% were 'poor' (Ref: Figure 7.3).

Chart 7.1

Customers's Perceived Sercive Quality

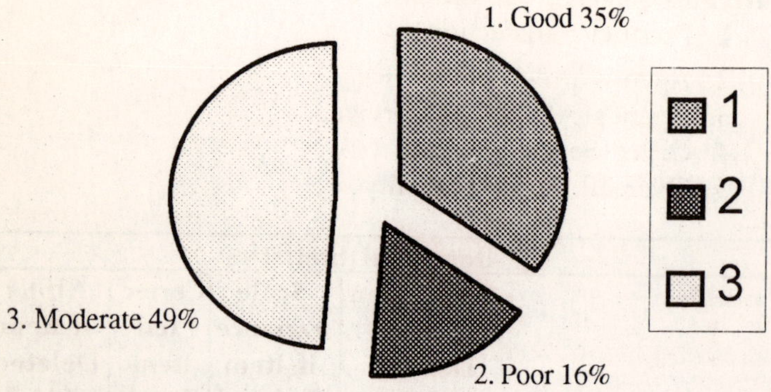

This shows that the total service quality in LIC is 'moderate' which could be the result of moderate satisfaction perceived by the customers on the LIC's policies, Agent's services, and the Office services. Secondly, the market itself is experiencing globalization, liberalization and reforms, which has resulted in heightened expectations of the LIC policyholders as well. Therefore, immediate and concrete efforts should be made by LIC on the followings:

- Developing a suitable mechanism to measure and monitor the service quality regularly at the operating offices,

- Obtaining customers' expectations about the various products, agent's services and the office services periodically, and the same must be incorporated into its internal evaluation systems so as to match the organisational efforts to the customers' expectations,
- Design Quality Improvement Programs on the lines of TQM and the same should be implemented more vigorously at the operating offices, and create a Quality Corporate Identity in the perception of the customers.

Summary

This index was developed using the multiple indicators of service quality, which include Product satisfaction, Agent's service, Office service, and over-all quality measures. This ensures a comprehensive measure of quality, which incorporates the linear relationship of the variables into the measurement. And, this index has also been found as a good loyalty predictor[4] since it is found maximizing the relationships between service quality and the customer behavioral responses (Loyalty).

REFERENCES

* The description of the variables used in the model is given below:

1 Agent's pre-sales service was measured using a five point scale on the following service items: Selection of policy, Counselling of financial needs, Knowledge and competency, explaining the benefits of various policies, Friendliness, Assistance in filling up the necessary forms, and Attentive to the customers.

2 Product satisfaction is average values of need satisfaction, cost, return, liquidity, and safety.

3 Agent's after-sales service was measured using a five point scale on the following items :

Reviewing the insurance needs of their clients, Assistance in remittance of premium, Assistance in premium notice, Assistance in policy documents, Assistance in other after-sales services.

4 Office service: The SERVPERF Score was used for office service.

5. Over-all service quality: A single item scale with very poor (1) to very good (5) was used.

6. For agent's service, a single measure was obtained by combining the pre-sales and after sales service measures of the agents.

7. All co-efficient alphas exceed the .70 level is recommended as an acceptable reliability by Nunnally (1978).

8. The variance extracted by the latent variable should be 50% or more (Fornell and Larcker (1981), Bagozzi and Yi (1988).

9. A measure, which maximises the relationship between service quality and customer behavioural responses (loyalty), is proved to be the better predictor of actual loyalty returns.

Chapter 8

SERVICE QUALITY AND CUSTOMERS' BEHAVIOURAL RESPONSES

Introduction

This chapter assesses the impact of service quality on customers' behavioral responses. It also measures the impact of service quality parameters: product satisfaction, agent's service, and office service, on the same behavioral response variables.

Service Quality and Customer Behavioral Responses

The review of literature suggests that the relationship of service quality and customers' behavioral responses[1] is very complex and difficult to understand as the equal number of studies have found this relationship as either 'linear' or 'non-exist'. The relationship is found to be varied upon the nature of the market (monopolistic/ competitive). To elaborate, customer satisfaction studies of Bolton and Drew(1991)[2]; Anderson, Fornell and Lehmann(1994)[3]; Kordupleski, Rust and Zahorik (1993)[4]; and Rust, Zahorik and Keininghm(1995)[5] have unanimously found that Quality is an investment and customer satisfaction and service quality have a measurable impact on customer retention, market share and profitability. Though many studies conclude that high customer satisfaction leads to high profitability, some reveal no such correlation among service quality, market share, and profitability. A study by the American Quality Foundation[6], and Ernst & Young,[7] suggests that many companies are wasting their efforts in trying to improve quality (American Quality Foundation 1992). The consulting firm of A.T. Kearney and Arthur D. Little[8] presents equally disappointing findings in two separate studies: These include (1) more than 80% of 100 British Firms reported "No significant impact as a result of Quality Improvements", and (2) Almost two thirds of 500 U.S. companies saw "Zero competitive gains" (The Economist 1992). However, the above studies did not indicate the type of firms (Manufacturing or Service industry).

The literature on Service Marketing strongly supports that there is a positive correlation between service quality and customer satisfaction and market share of a firm. Forenell (1992)[9] enumerates several key benefits of high customer satisfaction for a firm. In general, high customer satisfaction should indicate increased loyalty for current customers, reduced price elasticity, insulation of current customers from competitive efforts, lower cost of future transactions, reduced failure costs, lower cost of attracting new customers and enhanced reputation for the firm.

Significance of Service Quality on Loyalty

An increased loyalty of current customers means more customers repurchasing (be retained) in the future. If a firm has a strong customer loyalty, it should be reflected in the firm's economy, because it ensures a steady stream of future cash flow (Reichheld and Sasser 1990)[10].

The service quality should reduce price elasticity for current customers (Garvin 1988)[11]. The satisfied customers are more willing to pay for the benefits they receive and are more likely to be tolerant of increases in price. This implies high margins of profits and customer loyalty (Reichheld & Sasser 1990)[12]. Superior quality of service should lower the cost of transactions in the future. If a firm has high customer retention, it does not need to spend as much to acquire new customers each time. Satisfied customers are likely to buy more frequently and in greater volume and buy other goods and services offered by the firm (Reichheld and Sasser 1990)[13].

Consistently providing goods and services that satisfy customers should lead to increase profitability by reducing failure costs. A firm that consistently provides high customer satisfaction should have lesser resources devoted to handling returns, reworking defective items, and handling and managing complaints (Crosby 1979; Garvin 1988, TARP 1979, 1981)[14].

The costs of attracting new customers should be lower for firms that achieve a high level of service quality (Fornell 1992)[15]. For example, satisfied customers are more likely to engage in positive word of mouth, and less likely to engage in damaging negative word of mouth, for the firm (Anderson 1994b; Howard and Sheth 1969; Reichheld and Sasser 1990; TARP 1979, 1981)[16]. Media sources are also more likely to convey positive information to prospective buyers. Customer satisfaction claims may make the advertising more effective, and, high customer satisfaction may allow the firm to offer attractive warranties.

The superior service quality should also enhance the overall reputation (image) of the firm. An enhanced reputation may aid in introducing new products by providing instant awareness and lowering the buyer's risk of trial (Robertson and Gatignon 1986; Schmalansee 1978)[17]. Reputation can also be beneficial in establishing and maintaining relationships with key suppliers, distributors, and potential allies (Anderson and Weitz 1989; Montgomery 1975)[18]. Reputation can provide a halo effect for the firm that positively influences customer evaluations, providing insulation from short-term shocks in the environment. Customer satisfaction should play an important role in building other important assets for the firm, such as brand equity (Aaker 1992; Keller 1993)[19].

Service Quality and Life Insurance Business

Thus, the above discussed views of various researchers suggest that the superior service quality would result in positive word-of-mouth, more repurchase, more retention, higher organisational preference, reduced price elasticity and enhanced reputation for the firm. However, making such a simple linear assumption that the service quality would have a measurable impact on life insurance business in India, is highly hypothetical, because of the uniqueness of life insurance market which appears to have dual market environments: on one side, it is looked as a financial market with high competitive environment, and on the other side it is the life insurance with monopolistic nature of market. If life insurance is more of financial business (i.e. competitive market), the service quality would have a positive linear relationship on life insurance business, but the relationship might be for a short period of time. Further, if it is a pure life insurance (i.e. monopolistic market), the relationship may be linear, it might be a false loyalty because no alternative is available.

It has been earlier said that superior quality is more likely to create positive word of mouth, and less likely to have a negative word of mouth. But, in life insurance, it is highly testable, because the life insurance concept is highly abstract and the benefit is contingent in nature, therefore, service quality alone might not be sufficient to create voluntary recommendation. But the other school of thought is that life insurance is an intangible product, so the highly reliable service will only ensure the policyholders a confidence of getting the product benefits in the future. Hence, the superior quality would definitely be resulting into a positive word-of-mouth recommendation.

The second assumption is that the superior quality would result in more repurchase. But this again may be highly hypothetical in life insurance for three reasons: i) The monopolistic nature of market may cause a false relationship, ii) Since the need for insurance is latent, the demand may be less, and iii) life insurance selling is highly personal, so a strong persuasion of marketing people can make even a dissatisfied customer to go in for repurchase.

And the third notion is superior quality in an organisation would improve the retention of the customers and also provide high insulation from competitors' efforts. In life insurance, 'the degree of lapsation or surrender', is a good indicator of retention. The low degree of lapsation and surrender would indicate higher retention. Here again, since the reasons for lapsation and surrenders are many, it is expected that the effect of service quality might be less. The better service quality increases organisational patronage (even in a competitive market). But, whether it would have a significant effect on life insurance is also a hypothetical issue.

The last but not the least issue is that service quality should also enhance the image of the firm. But, it is yet to be tested in life insurance.

Setting the Hypotheses for validation

Although the superior service is likely to foster the favorable behavior and reduce the likelihood of unfavorable behavior, an important unresolved issue is: what service-quality level is required to have the desired impact on behaviors? How much service quality is enough to retain customers? Does the association between service quality and behavioral intentions change at different quality levels? Which components of service quality would be the most significant determinant on the behavioral intentions? All these questions have helped to form a series of hypotheses to test in this chapter.

In the literature, service quality has been defined mostly as a global concept formed out of the cumulative experience of a series of service encounters with a firm and is expected to have a positive linear relationship with the behavioral responses. This assumption has led to form a hypothesis (1): *"Service quality has a positive linear relationship on customers' behavioral responses"*.

The empirical analysis in the earlier chapters revealed that product satisfaction, agents service, office service, and overall service quality are all linearly related to the service quality Index. Therefore, the Index would be a good indicator of loyalty. This suggests to have an assumption that service quality would have a greater impact on the customers' behavioral responses, and its components (product satisfaction, agent's service and office service) would have separate and distinct effects on the behavioral responses. Hence, this led to study the Hypothesis (2): *"Service quality would have greater impact on customers' behavioral responses", and Hypothesis (3) "Product satisfaction, Agent's service, and Office service would have separate and distinct effects on customers' behavioral responses".*

It is expected that higher satisfaction would lead to positive behavioral responses (positive word-of-mouth communications, repurchase, more retention, improved image and loyalty) and dissatisfaction would lead to negative behavioral responses (negative word-of-mouth, no repurchases, lapsation / surrenders, decreased image and switch-over to other organisation). But the impact of dissatisfaction on behavioral responses would be much greater than satisfaction. Thus, one unit of dissatisfaction on an attribute could have a greater effect on the behavioral response variables than a corresponding unit of positive performance. This assumption has led to set the Hypothesis *(4):"Dissatisfaction would have greater impact on the customers' behavioral responses than satisfaction".*

Operationalisation of the variables

In this study, customers' behavioral responses were operationalised into the following five categories: 1) Word of mouth communication, 2) Re-purchase intentions, 3) Retention (NoSurrenders/Lapsations), 4) Organisational Preference, and 5) Company Image. The variables used in this analysis are given below:

I Description of independent variables:

I) Service quality: A Service Quality Index has been used as an indicator for service quality,

ii) Office Service: The SERVPERF score, which is the average perceived performance score across the ten dimensions was used for office service.

iii) Agent Service: An average value of the various agents' services was used for the agent's service.

iv) Product Satisfaction: The average score of need satisfaction + cost + return + liquidity + safety of the product was used for product satisfaction.

II. Description of the dependent variables (Behavioral Response variables)

I) *Word of mouth:* Word of mouth was operationalised as the extent of willingness to recommend LIC to others in a four point scale with the adjectives - Definitely No (1) to Definitely Yes (4).

ii) *Repurchase:* Repurchase was measured as likelihood of repurchase in the near future in four point scale with Definitely No (1) to Definitely Yes (4).

iii) *Retention:* This was measured in terms of both lapsation and surrenders. If any policy was surrendered a score of '1', otherwise '0' was given. Similarly if any policy was lapsed, a score of '1', otherwise '0' was assigned.

iv) *Preference:* It means 'preference of LIC over other organisations'. If LIC was preferred then a score of '1' was given, otherwise '0'

v) *Company Image:* LIC's image, on service quality, compared to other similar organisations was obtained in the form of rankings: If LIC was ranked first, a score of 1 has been given, otherwise '0'

Validity of the Hypotheses

Hypothesis (1): 'service quality has a positive linear relationship with customers' behavioral responses,' was tested by using a series of simple regressions separately where behavioral response variables are the dependent variables and service quality is the independent variable. However, to study the effect of the service quality on preference, image, lapsation and surrenders -'Logistic Regression' was used, mainly because the dependent variable is a two-category variable. The regression analysis has revealed the following results:

Service quality is found to have a positive linear relationship with all the behavioral response variables except lapsation. It has a greater impact on Image (B=0.82, W=30.11, P=. 00) and Preference (B=0.92, W=40.12, P=. 00). But on recommendation (B=0.35, t=7.33, P=. 00), and Repurchase (B=0.19, t=3.49, P=. 00), Its effects are moderate. On Surrenders (B=-0.42, W=4.89, P=. 05), the effect is negative as it is expected that higher service quality would reduce surrenders thereby increasing the retention, but its effect is not significant on Lapsation (B=-0.14, W=1.19, P=. 27) (Ref: Table 8.1).

Next Hypothesis (3) 'Product satisfaction, Agent's service, and Office service would have separate and distinctive effects on customers' behavioral responses', was tested first because hypothesis (2) is a comparative evaluation and partially depends on Hypothesis (3). To test the Hypothesis (3), separate multiple regressions were carried out with each of these behavioral response variables where the same (behavioral response variables) were regressed on product satisfaction, agent's service, and office service. The analysis has revealed that 'all these three components of service quality have separate and distinct effects on the behavioral response variables'.

Office service is found to have a greater impact on the behavioral responses over the others as it has significant relationship in almost all the behavioral variables except repurchase and lapsation. Thus, office service has more effect on Preference (B=0.80, W=17.20, P=. 00) and Image (B=0.63, W=10.19, P=. 001). But it has low effect on Recommendation (B=0.21, t=4.19, P=. 00) and moderate negative effect on Surrenders (B= -0.46, W=2.41, P=. 12) (Ref: Table 8.1)

Similarly, product satisfaction has strong effects on Preference (B=1.05, W=5.74, P=. 02), Image (B=1.33, W=8.27, P=. 004), and Lapsation (B= -1.01, W=4.57, P=. 03). But it has a low effect on Repurchase (B=0.11, t=2.16, P=. 03) and Recommendation (B=0.21, t= 4.14, P=. 00).

The agent's service has also low effects on Recommendation (B=0.14, t=2.76, P=. 006), and Preference (B=0.34, W=4.59, P=. 03) and in all other variables, its effects are insignificant (Ref: Table 8.1).

To test Hypothesis (2): 'Service quality would have greater impact on customers' behavioral responses', the impact of service quality was compared with that of the other three components (product satisfaction, agent's service, and office service) on the same behavioral responses. And, the impact of service quality has been found to be greater on the behavioral responses. The 't' value[20] also indicates that service quality has significant relationships in almost all the behavioral variables except lapsation where the product satisfaction has a greater impact (Ref: Table 8.1).

(H4) It is hypothesized that "Effect of Dissatisfaction on behavioral responses would be greater than satisfaction". To test this, Multiple Regression with dummy variables was performed where each of these behavioral variables was regressed on the dummy variables: satisfied, and dissatisfied.

Table 8.1

Impact of Product satisfaction, Agent's service, Office service, and Service Quality on the customer's behavioural responses:

Variables	Product satisfaction	Agent's service	Office service	Service Quality
1. Word-of-mouth	.0.21***	0.14***	0.21***	0.35***
(4.19)	(2.76)	(4.14)	(7.53)	
2. Repurchase	0.11**	0.06	0.07	0.19***
(2.16)	(1.05)	(1.39)	(3.49)	
3. Preference	1.05**	0.34**	0.80***	0.92***
(5.74)	(4.59)	(17.20)	(40.12)	
4. Image	1.33***	–0.01	0.63***	0.82***
(8.27)	(.002)	(10.19)	(30.11)	
5. Lapsation	–1.01**	0.02	0.02	–0.14
(4.57)	(.01)	(.01)	(1.19)	
6. Surrenders	–0.22	–0.22	–0.46*	–0.42**
(.08)	(.57)	(2.41)	(4.89)	

Note : (*) Figures in the parenthesis are the t/Wald statistics.

*** Indicates Significance at 1% level.

** Significance at 5% level.

* Significance at 10% level.

* Significance at 15% level.

Table 8.2

Effect of satisfaction/dissatisfaction on Customer's Behavioural responses :

Behavioural Response Variables	Product Satisfaction		Agent's Service		Office Service		Service Quality	
	Satisfied	Dissatisfied	Satisfied	Dissatisfied	Satisfied	Dissatisfied	Satisfied	Dissatisfied
1. Word-to-mouth	0.44^{*}	-0.07	0.24^{**}	-0.30^{*}	0.29^{***}	-0.32^{**}	0.36^{***}	-0.51^{***}
(1.79)	(-.26)	(2.09)	(-1.85)	-1.85)	(2.61)	(-2.14)	(3.34)	(3.54)
2. Repurchase	0.11	-0.44	-0.01	-0.15	0.12	-0.15	-0.09	-0.51^{***}
(.41)	(1.53)	(.04)	-.82)	(.98)	(-.90)	(.75)	(3.24)	
3. Preference	0.61	-0.24	0.40^{*}	-0.29	0.72^{***}	-1.02^{***}	0.89^{***}	-1.63^{***}
(1.19)	.16)	(2.61)	(.62)	(9.33)	(6.95)	(13.57)	(12.58)	
4. Lapsation	0.89	0.03	-0.004	-0.31	0.39^{*}	-1.30^{***}	0.55^{***}	-2.10^{***}
(1.88)	(.002)	(.0002)	(.68)	(2.66)	(7.88)	(11.70)	(5.20)	
5. Image	-0.44	0.17	0.16	0.25	0.03	0.25	0.11	0.60^{**}
(.55)	(.074)	(.28)	(.35)	(.011)	(.47)	0.12)	(2.86)	
6. Surrenders	-0.07	0.37	-0.38	0.35	-0.57	0.47	-1.27^{**}	0.31
(.01)	(.11)	(.62)	(.34)	(1.19)	(.77)	(3.84)	(.37)	

Note : Figures in the parenthesis (*) are the t/wald satistics.

* Indicates Significance at 10% level.

** Indicates Significance at 5% level.

*** Indicates Significance at 1% level.

Significance at 15% level.

Description of the dummy variables: The satisfied customers were given a value of '1' if satisfied, otherwise '0'. Similarly, in case of Dissatisfied customers, a value of '1', otherwise '0' were given. And, the moderate group was taken as a reference group. The analysis reveals that dissatisfaction has a greater impact on the behavioral response than satisfaction. Table (8.2) clearly shows that the effect of dissatisfaction is comparatively very high on almost all the behavioral response variables for service quality-almost one and half times more for word-of-mouth recommendation (-0.54 > 0.36)*, 5 times more for repurchase (-0.51 > -0.09). The dis-satisfaction effect is 3 to 5 times more for image (-2.10 > 0.55), preference (-1.63 > 0.89), and lapsation (0.60 > 0.11)[9]. However, in case of surrender, the effect of satisfaction is more (0.31* < -1.27).

For office service, the effect of dissatisfaction is more on preference (1.02 > 0.72), and image (1.30 > 0.39), and equal on word-of-mouth (0.32 > 0.29).

But for product satisfaction and agent's service the effects are different. In case of product satisfaction - the effect of dissatisfaction is more in repurchase (0.44 > 0.11), but, on word-of-mouth (0.07 < 0.44), and image (0.03 < 0.89) - satisfaction has greater effect. In case of agent's service, dissatisfaction has a greater impact on word-of-mouth (0.30 > 0.24), and satisfaction has more effect on preference (0.29 < 0.40).

Summary

The above results show that the Service Quality Index is a good predictor of loyalty as it is found to have a greater impact on almost all the loyalty indicators: word of mouth, repurchase, preference, image, lapsation and surrenders. Product satisfaction has also significant effects on certain variables i.e., preference, image, and lapsation. These results suggest that to have better Company Image and more retention of customers, these measures particularly the service quality index and the product satisfaction need to be regularly monitored and improved upon.

REFERENCES

* The values in the parentheses are Beta Coefficients. The former value indicates 'effect of dis-satisfaction' and the later indicates the 'effect of satisfaction' on the behavioural response variables.

a The co-efficient is not significant even at .15 confidence level.

1 Here, the term "customers' behavioral intentions" refers to the intended responses of customers to the perceived service quality of a firm.

2 Bolton, Ruth N., and James H. Drew (1991), "A Multistage Model of Customers' Assessments of Service Quality and Value," Journal of Consumer Research, 17 (March), P. 375-84.

3 Anderson, Eugene W., Claes Fornell, and Donald R. Lehmann (1994), "Customer Satisfaction, Market Share, and Profitability," Journal of Marketing, 58 (July), P. 53-66.

4 Ibid. P. 55.

5 Roland T. Rust, Anthony J. Zahorik, and L. Keiningham (1995), "Return on Quality (ROQ): Making Service Quality Financially Accountable," Journal of Marketing, 59 (April), P. 58-70.

6 American Quality Foundation (1992), Best Practices Report, Cleveland: Ernst and Young.

7 American Quality Foundation (1992).

8 Anderson, Eugene W. (1994), P. 53.

9 Claes Fornell (1992), "A National Customer Satisfaction Barometer: The Swedish Experience," Journal of Marketing, 55 (January), P. 6.

10 Reichheld, Fredrick F., and W. Earl Sasser (1990), " Zero Defections: Quality Comes to Services," Harvard Business Review, 68 (September-October), P. 105-108.

11 Garvin David A. (1988), Managing Quality: The Strategic and Competitive Edge, New York: The Free Press.

12 Reichheld and Sasser (1990), P.105-108.

13 Ibid. P. 105-108.

14 Forenell (1994), P. 55.

15 Forenell (1992), P. 6-21.

16 Forenell (1994), P. 55.

17 Ibid. P. 55.

18 Ibid. P. 55.

19 Ibid. P. 56.

20 For comparisons between the measures - t values are considered as better indicators as it exactly represents the true proportions of the measures than Beta Coefficients.

Chapter 9

SUGGESTIONS FOR PRODUCT SATISFACTION

Introduction

This chapter consists of conclusion of the study and future strategies for improvement of total service quality in life insurance.

Suggestions for Product Satisfaction

Based on the above findings of the study and discussions held with the executives of LIC, the following suggestions are made for improvement in life insurance:

Product Satisfaction

1. The premium amount for the life policy is determined based on 1) Mortality experience, 2) Management expenses, and 3) Investment income. The cost of the policy is reviewed by evaluating each of these components. Any favorable experience in any of these would result in both reductions in premium rates and better return on the policies. In case of the existing polices,

the surplus would result in improvement in bonus rates, and for the new policies it would result in reduction in the premium amount. Any improvement in the cost of product would be primarily based on the scope for improvement in the above components. Therefore, the suggestions of the same, are given on individual component-wise:

1. Mortality Experience

i). As the general mortality rate in the country has been improving, there is a necessity for LIC to periodically revise the mortality table once in five to ten years. For the periodical revision of the mortality table, it is essential to have an up-to-date mortality data of its policyholders, which would be possible through a networking of all offices using computers. This would certainly help in creation of a large database.

ii) To have a better mortality experience, it is important to have more good lives on the books of the LIC. This demands for strengthening the monitoring of underwriting practices of its offices. In this regard, the agent's practice should also be periodically monitored; particularly the agent's confidential report requires more scrutiny. Besides, intensive training should be provided at regular intervals to the underwriting staff and the sales force.

iii) It would be useful if the premium rates (without profit) of the policies are reviewed periodically, at least once in three years, taking into account the improvement in the investment income, mortality experience, and management expenses. If as a result of such reviews any reduction in the premium rates takes place, the benefit can be passed on to the policyholders to the extent it is fair and feasible.

2. Management Expenses

i) The management expenses of the LIC include commission and other expenses to agents, salary and other benefits to employees, and other management expenses. The review of expenses ratio during the last five years showed that the first year expense (New Business) ratio[1] and renewal expense ratio[2] are on the increase side. This indicates a greater scope for reduction in the operational cost, which can be achieved through cost control measure and also by improving the productivity of the employees. In this regard, it is desirable that the first year and renewal cost ratios should be brought down to 60% and 11% respectively as suggested by the Malhotra Committee.

ii) Efforts should be made to increase the business of new polices and improve the retention of the inforce-polices to a greater level.

iii) Total computerization of various functions of offices would also certainly help in reducing the cost in the long run.

iv) It is suggested that, if more value added benefits like providing periodical installment of premium income on endowment polices, switch-over option to other plans, introduction of flexible, and universal products, etc., are added to the existing product benefits, it would help to create a perception of low cost or greater product satisfaction among the policyholders.

v) Diversification into new areas such as Health insurance, Pension, Banking, Credit card, Merchant banking, Leasing etc., may help in increasing the business and re-deployment of its excess staff to these new offices. This also would help in reduction of cost to a greater extent.

vi) Though there is not much scope for reduction in marketing expenses, the agents may be motivated to improve the retention of inforce-polices that would result in higher Cost/Benefit ratio.

3. *Investment Income*

Investment income plays a vital role in reducing the cost of the product and increasing the bonus rates of the policies. In this regard, the following suggestions are made;

i) Regarding LIC's investment, section 27 of the Insurance Act permits it to invest its life fund in the following order: 75% of its life fund should be invested in the Central Government, State Government Securities, and Socially Oriented Sectors. In this respect, the Malhotra Committee suggested a change: "The investment of LIC should confirm to the broad pattern laid down in section 27 of the Insurance Act, subject to the modification indicated below:

ii) In Central Government securities being not less than 20%; (ii) In State Government securities and government guaranteed securities, inclusive of (a) above, being not less than 40%; (iii) In socially oriented sectors as may be prescribed by the Government from time to time inclusive of (b) above, being not less than 50%; (d) The rest 50% of the fund may be invested in the approved investments". Accordingly, LIC is suggested to make prudent investment decisions according to the financial market conditions prevailing from time to time while investing in the approved securities.

Other suggestions

i) Life insurance policies need to be positioned on the basis of its product features after proper segmentation. For instance, Endowment policies or Money Back policies should be positioned mainly on its unique financial features while term insurance polices viz. Bima Kiran, etc., should be positioned using its risk feature. And efforts should be made to improve the corporate image.

ii) Developing more number of financial products like unit-linked insurance etc. would improve its financial stake and corporate image.

iii) The liquidity aspects of certain polices like endowment, etc., need improvement, as the life policies are perceived to have poor liquidity. In this regard, introducing some short-term financial products would improve the perception.

Agent's Services

The suggestions to improve the agents' services are made as under:

1. Efforts should be made to improve the agent's counseling and presentation skills, and develop versatile product knowledge of the popular financial products. More input on these areas should be included in the training programmes specially designed for them.

2. They should be nurtured to explain the important benefits of various plans to their clients at the time of selling the policies.

3. Agents' friendliness with the clients needs improvement.

4. Development of professionalism among the agents should receive the prime attention, and selection of agents needs a review. Importance should be given for the individual's personal traits, flair for selling the products, and servicing skills at the time of their recruitment.

5. Agents are paid renewal commission mainly for improving the retention of the inforce-policies and for providing satisfactory after-sales services to their clients. But, it has been found that many of the agents do not turn-up to their clients after selling the policies. Therefore, it has been suggested that the Branch Managers should periodically monitor agent's service quality. In this regard, a standardized instrument measuring all aspects of agent's service has to be developed and customer response should be collected by using the instrument. Then, these data must be used as a basis for the payment of renewal commission to the agents. Thus, the renewal commission will become payable only when the agents get a satisfactory customer rating. This will compel the agents to provide satisfactory services to their clients.

6. Though all aspects of the agent's servicing need improvement, priorities should be given to "timely sending of premium notices, timely assistance in remittance of premium" as they were perceived as the very important factors in the study.

7. In the areas of review of clients' needs, responsiveness, assistance in rendering the intermediary services such as payment of loan, survival benefits, and maturity claims, etc., and agent's servicing require improvement. More importantly, the agents should be advised to have regular contacts with their clients.

8. More emphasis on 'relationship marketing' should be given in the agents' training.

9. Training to agents should be strengthened and the image of the sales training centers of LIC has to be improved. Selection of agents for this training has to be streamlined.

Office Services

The following suggestions have been made for improvements at the operating offices of LIC:

(1). In urban areas, Empathy factor should be given more importance. Regarding this, the following are suggested:

i. In training, more emphasis should be given on the service personnel including receptionists, sub-staffs, and attendants, on improving their behavioral responses to customers. This includes the ways of understanding the customers' needs, importance given to individual attention and valuing the customers, and developing of inter-personal skills.

ii. Suitable mechanism to efficiently tailor the service to customer's specific requirements needs to be developed. This often involves developing a computerized information system that captures customers' preferences and specific requirements and creates the opportunity for a more personalised and enhanced service quality, which would help in building-up the relationship with the customers.

(2). Responsiveness factor may receive secondary importance in urban areas, but in rural areas, it has to be given a prime recognition. A wide span-of action program needs to be designed to enhance the willingness and ability of the employees to be responsive to the customers' requirements. Such actions include:

i) Providing technical skills, customer related skills, and problem-solving skills;

ii) Empowering employees to exercise judgment and creativity in responding to the customer's special needs.

However, after such training and empowerment, the employees' performance has to be monitored periodically.

(3). The other service dimensions, which were rated high in importance by the customers, are *Reliability, Communication, Access, and System*. To improve the perception levels of the customers on these dimensions, the LIC should prepare certain action programs like:

i. Developing a value system for quality at all levels of the organisation, for example, by establishing reliability standard like PONC (Price of Non-Conformance), as a measure suggested by Philip Crosby,

ii. Teaching "why" and "how" of Reliability in the training programmes of the service personnel,

iii. Forming 'Reliability Teams' to evaluate specific services for ways to reduce failures,

iv. Measuring failure rates - number of mistakes per policy or average number of mistakes (in percentage) per particular time period (either quarterly or yearly),

v. Recognizing failure-free service,

vi. Minimizing the need for recovery service; which includes correcting the wrong service rendered, attending to the complaints or redressing the grievances,

vii. The service systems and procedures at the branch office need to be simplified. Regarding this, Re-engineering the service process and system is suggested.

(4). Infrastructure (tangibility) of the offices particularly in urban areas has to be improved. In the offices where certain necessary facilities like drinking water, seating arrangements, fans, toilets, etc., are found inadequate, necessary care should be taken to fill up the gaps. Installation of ATM and Voice Responsive System may help in improving the tangibility dimension.

(5). Organisational competence in the perception of customers needs to be improved. Regarding this, efforts should be made to improve the corporate image of LIC. The improvement efforts of the organization should be periodically published to the public, and LIC should be projected as a 'customer friendly organisation'.

(6). Internal Inspection System has to be made in conformance with the customer data.

(7). The important service dimensions such as Empathy, Responsiveness, Reliability, Tangibility, etc., have to be formulated into Key Performance Indicators (KPI). Then, the branch achievements on KPI need to be periodically measured, through customers' perceptions. For this purpose, Divisional offices of LIC should conduct a periodical survey of some selected customers of its branches by using the standardised instrument (SERVPERF). The results should be brought to the notice of all the branches. By using this data, the Best Branch, Best Department, and Best Service Person may be selected who may be honoured with an appreciation letter and certain financial incentives.

Service Quality Model and Index

1. The inter-relationships of the service quality parameters suggest a need to develop a model to study these inter-relationships which would help in studying the effects of one on another, and in prioritising the improvement efforts.

2. The service quality index used in this study suggests that, since the service quality parameters are linearly related to each other, and they are

interdependent, service quality of an organisation needs to be measured in totality with the help of such index. This would be a reliable quality measure general enough to be comparable, and benchmark across the operating offices of LIC.

Impact of Service Quality on Customer's Behavioral Responses

1. The Service Quality Index is a good predictor of loyalty as it is found to have a greater impact on almost all the loyalty indicators: word of mouth, repurchase, preference, image, lapsation and surrenders. Therefore, it can be used for studying the impact of the quality improvements on the customer's behavioral response variables, and also for cost-benefit analysis.

2. The customer's behavioral response data can be used to identify the loyal customers and also the customers who are likely to leave the corporation. This can help the organization to work out appropriate loyalty programs to increase the retention of the customers.

3. Product satisfaction also has significant effects on preference, image, and lapsation. The study results suggest that, to have a better company image and more customer retention, these measures, particularly the service quality index and product satisfaction, need to be regularly monitored and improved.

All these suggestions would help LIC in achieving 'Total Customer Satisfaction'.

Conclusion

Life insurance is expected to be opened up soon. The customers of LIC would demand for high quality service due to their heightened expectations, which would be a new challenge for the corporation. This demands for 'Quality Orientation' Programme. Secondly, life insurance servicing requires a triangle management of product, agent, and office, to deliver satisfactory service. And, these three quality parameters are interrelated. Hence, to understand the relationship between parameters and service quality, *a service quality model incorporating the linear relationships among the service quality parameters* is a must. The model developed by the authors indicates that, the parameters of service quality: product satisfaction, agent's service, office service, and over-all service quality are all linearly related to each other. This would enable the management to understand and monitor the service quality parameters.

Assessing the service quality in life insurance would be a more complex and difficult task, if the key factors determining the satisfaction of the quality parameters and the extent of their influence on service quality were not known. So, this study measures the key parameters of service quality (Product, Agent's service and Office service), and also identifies the factors determining the satisfaction of each parameter. This analysis indicates that customers' perceptions of all the quality parameters are mere 'moderate'. This analysis would enable LIC to know customer satisfaction of its key parameters, and the factors determining their satisfactions, which would also help in prioritising the quality improvement efforts.

In this study, the service quality is defined as *'customers' perceived service quality of all features and characteristics of product, service and people which gives total satisfaction'*. This led to measuring the service quality through customers' perceptions using multiple measures: Product, Agents service, Office service and over-all service quality. For this purpose, a linearly weighted composite index was developed. This helped to measure the customers' perceived service quality in LIC in accordance with its theoretical comprehensives. This index can be useful to measure service quality in totality and also to benchmark quality across the operating offices of LIC. Moreover, this index has been found as a good predictor of loyalty, which can be used to study the relationship of quality and loyalty.

Review of literature on this subject, indicated that the relationship between service quality and customer's behavioural response (Loyalty) is very complex and difficult to understand as equal numbers of studies have also found this relationship as either linear or non-linear. In India, particularly in life insurance, no such study has been done, and the relationship appears to be varying upon the nature of market (monopolistic/competitive). Life insurance, though appeared to be a monopolistic market, in the real sense, has been facing competition from other financial institutions. Therefore, the relationship of service quality and the behavioural responses of customers in life insurance have been studied. This analysis has indicated that service quality has a greater impact on all the behavioural response variables. The effect of dis-satisfaction is very high on these variables. This analysis would enable LIC i) to measure the impact of service quality on loyalty, ii) to identify loyal customers, and iii) to design loyalty improvement programmes to keep their loyal customers for a longer period of time.

In the end, it is hoped that the study conducted by the authors on Service Quality in life insurance in India would help the LIC and potential competitors to work out strategies for better customer service. Towards this end, they have a long way to go.

REFERENCES

1 New Business ratio: This is the ratio of the expenses incurred in the first year on account of procurement of new business to the first year premium income.

2 Renewal Expense ratio: This is the ratio of the renewal expenses to the premium income of inforce-polices.

BIBLIOGRAPHY

A. Book

1. Arthur Aron, Elaine N. Aron (1997), Statistics for the Behavioral and Social Sciences, New Jersey: Prentice-Hall, Inc.
2. Anthony S. Bryk ' and Stephen W. Raudenbush (1992), Hierarchical Linear Models, New Delhi. Sage Publications.
3. Benjarnin Schneider and David E. Bowen (1995), Winning the Service Game, Boston: Harvard Business School Press.
4. Dennis Green (1996), The complete ISO 9000 Manual, London: Kogan Page Ltd.
5. Edward G. Carmines, and Richard A. Zeller (1979), Reliability and Validity Assessment, New Delhi: Sage Publications.
6. Frederick F. Reichheld (1996), The Loyalty Effect, Boston: Harvard Business School Press.
7. Fred N. Kerlinger (1986), Foundation of Behavioral Research, New York: Harcourt Brace Jovanovich College Publishers.
8. Gummesson E. (1991), "Service Quality - A Holistic View," in Service Quality: Multidisciplinary and Multinational Perspectives, Brown S.W., Gummesson E., Edvardsson E., and Gustavsson B. (eds.), Lexington, MA: Lexington Books.
9. Insurance Institute of India (1987), Principles and Practice of Life Insurance, Study Course, Bombay.

10. Juran J.M. (1988), Planning for Quality, New York: The Free Press.
11. John J. Sviokla and Benson P. Shapiro (1992), Keeping Customer, Boston: Harvard Business School Press.
12. John P. Mclver, and Edward G. CarMines (1981), Uni-Dimensional Scaling, New Delhi: Sage Publications.
13. John P. Mclver, and Edward G. Carrnines (1981), Multi-Dimensional Scaling, New Delhi: Sage Publications.
14. Jill Griffin (1995), Customer Loyalty, New York: Lexington Books.
15. Johnson A. Edosomwan (1995), Customer and Market-Driven Quality Management, New Delhi: Tata McGraw-Hill Publishing Company Ltd.
16. Life Insurance Corporation of India (1991), Tryst with Trust: The LIC story, Kumar D (ed.), Bombay.
17. Michael S. Lewis-Beck (1993), Regression Analysis, New Delhi: Sage Publications.
18. Michael S. Lewis-Beck (1994), Factor Analysis and Related Techniques, New Delhi: Sage Publications.
19. Milind M. Lele, and Jagdish N. Sheth (1987), The Customer is Key, New York: John Wiley & sons, Inc.

Philip Crosby (1993), Quality is Free. New York: McGraw Hill, Inc.

Philip Crosby (1996), Quality is Still Free: Making Quality Certain in Uncertain Times, New York: McGraw Hill, Inc.

22 Ravi Shankar, "services Marketing - Some Conceptual Issues,' in Services Marketing: The Indian Experience, New Delhi.

23. Richard Tabor Greene (1993), Global Quality, Milwaukee: ASQC Quality Press.
24. Richard B. Darlington (1990), Regression and Linear Models, NewYork: McGraw-Hill Publishing Company.
25. Stamatis D.H. (1996), Total Quality Service, Florida: St. Lucie Press.
26. Tom Peters and Nancy Austin (1986), A Passion for Excellence, New York: Warner Books.

27. Valarie A. Zeithaml, Parasuraman A., and Leonard L. Barry (1990), Delivering Quality Service: Balancing Customer Perceptions and Expectations, New York: The Free Press.
28. Valarie A. Zeithaml, Parasuraman A., and Leonard L. Barry (1991), Marketing Services: Competing Through Quality, New York: The Free Press.

B. Reports

1. 'Committee on Reforms in Insurance Sector' (1994), submitted to the Ministry of Finance, Department of Economic Affairs, Insurance Division, New Delhi.
2. 'Quality Management in Service Organisations' (1993), by Evert Gummesson, ISQA, Sweden.
3. 'Vision 2001: Service Management and Image Building' (1997), GIC Mumbai.
4. 'Buyers and Non-Buyers in the Sales Process' (1990), A Study Report by LIMRA.
5. 'Vision 2001: Portents, Potentials and Proposed Plans' (1997), LIC Corporate Planning Department, Central Office, Mumbai.
6. American Quality Foundation (1992), Best Practices Report, Cleveland Ernst and Young.
7. Life Insurance Corporation of India, Agents Manual, Bombay.
8. Life Insurance Corporation of India, Annual Report of LIC 1996-97, Mumbai.

C. Articles in Journals

1 Akshay R. Rao, and Robert W. Ruekert (1994), "Brand Alliances as Signals of Product Quality," Sloan Management Review, (Fall), P. 87-97.

2 Anand Kasturi (1996), "Are You Being Served?" Management Review, (January-March), P. 40-49.

3 Anderson, EugeneW., Claes Fornell, and Donald R. Lehmann (1994), "Customer Satisfaction, Market Share, and Profitability, Journal of Marketing, 58 (July), P. 53-66

4 Anita Van de Vliet (1997), "Best Practice - Are they being served?" Management Today, (February) P. 66-72.

5 Babakus, and W. Glenn Mangold (1992), "Adapting the SERVQUAL Scale to Hospital Services : An Empirical Investigation, "Health Service Research, 26(6), P. 767-80.

6 Babakus, Emin, and Gregory W. Boller (1992), "An Empirical Assessment of the Servqual Scale," Journal of Business Research, 24, P. 253-68.

7 Bolton, Ruth N. and James H. Drew (1991) A Longitudinal Analysis of the Impact of Service Changes on Customer Attitudes," Journal of Marketing, 55 (January), P. 1-9.

8 Bolton, Ruth N., and James H. Drew (1991), "A Multistage Model of Customers' Assessments of Service Quality and Value, Journal of Consumer Research, 17 (March), P. 375-84.

9 Bradley T. Gale (1995), "Providing Superior Value," World Executive's Digest, (June), P. 33-38.

10 Brenda, and Bill Mullins (1992), '.'Does Your Company Fill-in the Blanks?" Canadian Insurance, (October), P. 9-12.

11 Brown, Stephen W., and Teresa A. Swartz (1989), "A Gap Analysis of Professional Service Quality," Journal of Marketing, 53 (April), P. 92-98.

12 Brown, Tom J., Gilbert A. Churchill, Jr., and J.Paul Peter (1993), "Improving the Measurement of Service Quality," Journal of Retailing, 69 (Spring), P. 127-39

13 Cadotte, Ernest R., Robert B. Woodruff, and Roger L. Jenkins (1987), "Expectations and Norms in Models of Consumer Satisfaction," Journal of Marketing Research, 24 (August), P. 305-14.

14 Carman James M. (1990), "Consumer Perceptions of Service Quality: An Assessment of the SERVQUAL Dimensions," Journal of Retailing, 66 (Spring), P. 33-55.

15 Charles R. Weiser (1995), "Championing the Customer," Harvard Business Review' (November'-December), P. 113-17.

16 Christopher W.C. Hart (1988), "The Power of Unconditional Service Guarantees," Harvard Business Review, (July-August).

17 Churchill, Gilbert A., and Carol Suprenant (1982), "An Investigation into the Determinants of Customer Satisfaction," Journal of marketing Research, 19 (November), P. 491-504.

18 Claes Fornell (1992), "A National Customer Satisfaction Barometer: The Swedish Experience," Journal of marketing, 55 (January), P. 1-21.

19 Claes Fornell, Michael D. Johnson, Eugene W. Anderson, Jaesung Cha, and Barbara Everitt Bryant (1996), "The American Customer Satisfaction Index: Nature, Purpose, and Findings," Journal of Marketing, 60 (October), P. 7-18.

20 Cronin J Joseph, Jr., and Steven A. Taylor (1994), 'SERVPEPF Versus SERVQUAL: Reconciling Performance-Based and Perceptions-Minus-Expectations Measurement of Service Quality," Journal of Marketing. 58 (January), P. 125-31.

21 Cronin J. Joseph, Jr., and Steven A. Taylor (1992), "Measuring Service Quality: A Reexamination and Extension," Journal of Marketing, 56 (July), P. 55-68.

22 Evert Gummesson (1991), "Truths and Myths in Service Quality," International Journal of Service Industry Management 2 (3), P. 7-16.

23 Howard E. Butz, Jr., Leonard D. Goodstein, "Measuring Customer Value: Gaining the Strategic Advantage," Organizational Dynamics, P. 63-77.

24 James L. Heskett, Thomas 0. Jones, Gary W. Loveman, W. Earl Sasser, Jr., and Leonard A. Schlesinger (1994), "Putting the Service-Profit Chain to Work," Harvard Business Review, (March-April), P. 164-75.

25 John R. Hauser and Don Clausing (1988), "The House of Quality," Harvard Business Review, (May-June).

26 Joseph B. Pine II, Don Peppers, and Martha Rogers (1995), "Do You Want to Keep Your Customers forever?", Harvard Business Review, (March-April), P. 103-15.

27 Kenneth Teas R. (1994), "Expectations as a Comparison Standard in Measuring Service Quality: An Assessment of a Reassessment," Journal of Marketing, 58 (January), P. 132-139.

28 Leonard L. Berry, and Parasuraman A. (1997), "Listening to the Customer - The Concept of a Service Quality Information System," Sloan Management Review, (Spring), P. 65-76.

29 Leonard L. Berry, Valarie A. Zeithaml, and Parasuraman A. (1990), "Five Imperatives for Improving Service Quality," Sloan Management Review, (Summer), P. 29-38.

30 Lester E. Coleman, and Denold G. Reynolds (1995), "The Voice of the Customer," World Executive's Digest, (February), P. 50-52.

31 Marugan P. (1996), "Quality of Service in State transport undertakings -Evaluations and Improvements Indian Journal of Transport Management, (July), 20 (7), P.

32 Mary Jo Bitner (1992), "Servicescapes: The Impact of physical Surroundings on Customers and Employees," Journal of Marketing, 56 (April), P. 57-71.

33 Michael D. Hartline and O.C. Ferrell (1996), "The Management of Customer- Contact Service Employees: An Empirical Investigation," Journal of marketing, 60 (October), P. 52-70.

34 Oliva, Terence A., Richard L.Oliver, and lan C. MacMillan (1992), "A Catastrophe Model for Developing Service Satisfaction Strategies," Journal of Marketing, 56 (July), P. 83-95.

35 Oliver, Richard L. (1980), "A Cognitive Model of the Antecedents and Consequences of Satisfaction Decisions," Journal of Marketing Research, 17 (November), P. 460-69.

36 James (1995), "The Reality of Customer Service," National Insurance News, P. 50-53.

37 Parasuraman A., Leonard L. Berry and Valarie A. Zeithaml (1991), "Understanding Customer Expectations of Service,"

Sloan Management Review, 32 (spring), P. 39-48.

38 Parasuraman A., Leonard L. Berry, and Valarie A. Zeithaml (1994), "Reassessment of Expectations as a comparison Standard in Measuring Service Quality: Implications for further Research," Journal of marketing, 58 (January), P 111-24.

39 Parasuraman A., Valarie A. Zeithaml and Leonard L. Berry (1991), "Refinement and Reassessment of the SERVQUAL Scale," Journal of Retailing, 67 (4) P. 420-50

40 Parasuraman A., Valarie A. Zeithaml, and Leonard Berry (1985), "A Conceptual Model of Service Quality and its Implications for Further Research," Journal of Marketing, 48 (Fall), P. 41-50.

41 Parasuraman A., Valarie A. Zeithaml, and Leonard Berry (1985), "SERVQUAL: A Multiple-Item Scale for Measuring Consumer Perceptions of Service," Journal of Retailing, 64 (Spring), P. 12-40.

42 Reichheld, Fredrick F., and W.Earl Sasser (1990),"Zero Defections: Quality Comes to Services," Harvard Business Review, 68 (September-October), P. 105-11.

43 Richard A. Spreng, Scott B. MacKenzie, and Richard W. Olshavsky (1996), "A Reexamination of the Determinants of Consumer Satisfaction," Journal of Marketing, 60 (July), P. 15-32.

44 Richard T. Watson (1998), "Measuring Information Systems Service Quality: Lessons From Two Longitudinal Case Studies," Management of Information Science Quarterly, (March), P. 61-75.

45 Roland T. Rust, Anthony J. Zahorik, and L. Keiningham (1995), "Return on Quality (ROQ): Making Service Quality Financially Accountable," Journal of Marketing, 59 (April), P. 58-70.

46 Sanjeev Varki and Roland T. Rust (1997), Satisfaction is Relative," Marketing Research, (Summer), 9 (2), P. 15-19.

47 Steven Albrecht (1996), "See Things from the Customer's Point of view," World Executive's Digest, (December), P. 53-58.

48 Steven E. Prokesch (1995), "Competing on Customer Service," An Interview with British Airways - Sir Colin Marshall," Harvard Business Review, (November - December), P. 101-112.

49 Steward G. Doss (1995), "Distribution System in LIC-A Review," Dnyanajyoti, (December), 12 (2), P. 5-17.

50 Susan M. Keaveney (1995), Customer Switching Behavior in Service Industries: An Exploratory Study," Journal of marketing, 59 (April), P. 71-82.

51 Teas, R. Kenneth (1993), "Expectations, Performance Evaluation, and Consumer Perceptions of Quality," Journal of Marketing, 57 (October), P. 18-34.

52 Thomas 0. Jones, and W. Earl Sasser, Jr. (1995), "Why satisfied Customers Defect" Harvard Business Review, 73 (November-December), P. 88-99.

53 Valarie A. Zeithaml, Leonard L. Berry, and Parasuraman A. (1996), "The Behavioral Consequences of Service Quality," Journal of Marketing, 60(April), P. 31-46.

54 Vikas Mittal, William T.Ross, Jr., and Patrick M. Houston (1998), "The Asymmetric impact of Negative and Positive Attribute-Level Performance on Over-all Satisfaction and Repurchase Intentions," Journal of Marketing, 62 (January), P. 33-47.

55 Zohorik, Anthony J. and Roland T. Rust (1992), "Modeling the Impact of Service Quality on Profitability: A Review," in Advances in Service Marketing and Management, T. Swartz (ed.), Greenwich CT: JAI Press, P. 247-76.

●●●